TEN CENTS
on the
DOLLAR

OR THE BANKRUPTCY GAME

TEN CENTS
on the
DOLLAR

OR THE BANKRUPTCY GAME

SIDNEY RUTBERG

BeardBooks

Washington, D.C.

Library of Congress Cataloging-in-Publication Data

Rutberg, Sidney.
  Ten cents on the dollar, or, The bankruptcy game / by Sidney Rutberg.
        p.   cm.
  Originally published: New York : Simon & Schuster, 1973.
  ISBN 1-893122-31-X (pbk.)
  1. Bankruptcy–United States. I. Title II. Title: Ten cents on the dollar.
III. Title: Bankruptcy game.
HG3766.R87   1999
332.7 ' 5 ' 0973--dc21   99-39393
                                                                   CIP

To Adele, Allen,
and all my friends
in the credit and bankruptcy fraternity

Contents

INTRODUCTION TO BANKRUPTCY   9

1 · A Kipper Is Not a Herring   15
BANKRUPTCY AUCTION SALES AND HOW THEY'RE
RIGGED

2 · Cheaper than Wholesale   28
JUICY BANKRUPTCY FRAUDS

3 · Ten Cents on the Dollar, or Reading Between
the Lies   45
BEHIND THE SCENES AT A CREDITORS' MEETING

4 · You Have to Give a Bankrupt Credit   61
THE CARE AND FEEDING OF THE CREDIT MAN IN
THE BANKRUPTCY FIELD

5 · Bankruptcies Add Up for Accountants   71
THE ACCOUNTANT WHO SPECIALIZES IN BANK-
RUPTCIES AND HOW HE GETS THE BUSINESS

6 • Why Bankruptcy Lawyers Never Go Bankrupt   86
WHAT THE LAWYERS DO, WHO THEY ARE AND HOW
MUCH MONEY THEY MAKE

7 • Through the Swinging Courtroom Doors   111
HOW INDIVIDUAL BANKRUPTCIES ARE HANDLED

8 • Arrangement or Reorganization   129
CHAPTER X AND CHAPTER XI OF THE BANKRUPTCY
ACT AND OUT-OF-COURT SETTLEMENTS

9 • Even Millionaires Go Broke   151
THE STORY OF LAMMOT DU PONT COPELAND, JR.

10 • Bankruptcy—Wall Street Style   165
BLOODBATH IN THE BROKERAGE BUSINESS

11 • How to Spot a Bust   180
DISTANT EARLY-WARNING SIGNALS

Introduction to Bankruptcy

In ancient Rome, bankruptcy was punishable by slavery or death, and when creditors disagreed on the alternative, the bankrupt could be dismembered, with each creditor claiming his portion. In Italy today, bankruptcy is cited as legal evidence of moral turpitude.

Here in modern America, bankruptcy is no great honor, but it is no longer a disgrace. In the land of the hard sell and the easy credit, bankruptcy is an everyday, almost socially acceptable system of getting out from under an unmanageable debt load.

A man earning $200 a week cannot realistically be expected to pay off $500,000 in debts, and a business that owes a million dollars can't pay up if its assets are only $100,000. Yet in our credit-card society, this kind of debt-to-earnings or debt-to-assets ratio turns up all too frequently. It's around such circumstances that the bankruptcy game is played.

In addition to wiping out debt, bankruptcy proceedings are carefully contrived to see that whatever assets are available are distributed fairly. But in practice, the assets serve essentially as a reservoir for the enrichment of a select group of professionals—lawyers, accountants, auctioneers, appraisers, *et al.*

Professionals who play the bankruptcy game are no more honest or dishonest than those in the used-car business or dry cleaning or fruits and vegetables or investment banking. They lie a little, they cheat a little, they steal a little, but mostly they work hard.

The fees in a bankruptcy case get paid before anyone else sees a dime. There is a complicated system of priorities for payment of taxes, wages, secured claims and the like, and way down on the bottom of the pile is the poor general creditor. He's the one who sold merchandise or lent money to a business before it went into bankruptcy, and in most cases there's little or nothing for him.

The bankrupts themselves generally fall into two categories—the honest shnook who gets into debt over his head through bad judgment or unfortunate circumstances and the cool professional bankrupt who knows precisely what he's doing, runs up a mountain of debts and then hurries to the bankruptcy courts where he can thumb his nose at angry and frustrated creditors.

The corporation is the bankrupt's best friend. Under the Bankruptcy Act, an individual can go to court to have his debts wiped out only once every six years. But with the judicious use of the corporate form, it's possible for the same individual to take a different corporation into bankruptcy every day. I don't know of anyone with that kind of track record, but there are "professional bankrupts" who seem to turn up with remarkable frequency as officers and stockholders of corporations that find their way into the bankruptcy courts. For them bankruptcy has become a way of life and a vehicle for fun and profits.

But most businessmen who go bankrupt must be dragged in. They fight it with all their strength, and when they finally succumb they find it bewildering and humiliating. Individuals who go bankrupt—and these far outnumber business bankruptcies—are usually victims trapped by the lure of easy credit, though here again there are the deadbeats and the hustlers who take advantage of bankruptcy for their own benefit.

The typical honest business bankruptcy might arise like this:

A manufacturer decides that long skirts are going to sell big and makes up a warehouseful. The season comes and the girls want short skirts. He can't move his inventory, and his piece-goods suppliers are screaming for money. He goes to a finance company, borrows against his accounts receivable and pays off some of his debts. Meanwhile, he's got to pay high interest rates on the finance-company loan, his inventory still isn't moving and overhead expenses are draining away his capital. He'll go to his relatives and borrow more to pay off creditors who scream the loudest. Then the season is over and he has his warehouseful of long dresses. He's forced to sell them for a fraction of cost and finds he still owes more than he can pay. Bankruptcy may be the only way out.

Then there's the phony who goes into business with bankruptcy in mind. He puts in some money and starts buying like mad. Everything from bicycles to baby powder. He pays at first and establishes a credit rating. He buys in ever increasing quantities and, as soon as the stuff arrives, resells it for cash at less than his cost. This sounds like a dumb way to do business, but it's not so dumb if he pockets the proceeds and doesn't pay for the merchandise. Instead he goes to court and declares bankruptcy.

The creditors are enraged, but if they can't prove the whole thing was a plot—and proof is not easy to come by—the promoter goes free and the creditors wind up with a bad case of heartburn. If the bankrupt is a real pro, he'll leave some assets to cover the expenses of administration, but never anything for the creditors. Known in the trade as an overbuy, the promotion of this kind of fraudulent bankruptcy is a favorite among racketeers who find bankruptcy sometimes as profitable as gambling, dope peddling or loan sharking.

While bankruptcy generally marks the end of a business, there are several forms of near bankruptcy in which an ailing business might be reorganized so it can continue. There are those two confusing chapters—Chapter X and Chapter XI. In my experience covering the bankruptcy courts, probably no question came up as frequently as "What's the difference between Chapter X and Chapter XI?" There are a number of differences which I'll go into later. But probably the most important is how the fees are passed out.

Under Chapter XI, the lawyer for the financially troubled company will get the biggest fee in the case. Under Chapter X, the court immediately appoints a trustee (generally a political payoff) and the trustee picks a lawyer. The big money in the Chapter X goes to the trustee and his attorney, while the lawyer who brought the case to court in the first place is shunted off to a role of a spectator. So you'll find a strong preference among bankruptcy lawyers for Chapter XI.

Both are designed to give a sick business court protection until it is nursed back to health or is declared hopeless and liquidated.

There is another form of near bankruptcy that rarely makes the newspapers but is quite common, particularly in textile, apparel and retail fields. This is the common-law, or out-of-court settlements. Many of the lawyers and accountants regard this as the best way to handle a failing business. For one thing, there's no court supervision of the fees or of anything else. The procedure boils down to a negotiating situation with the debtor company trying to pay as little as it can get away with and the creditors trying to salvage as much as possible.

On the question of fees, the creditors—or, more precisely, the credit men for the creditor companies—decide how much is paid. Thus we find some interesting relationships springing up among credit men and bankruptcy lawyers and accountants.

The credit man is a key player in the bankruptcy game. In fact he's usually the one who blows the whistle to get the game started. The credit man's function is to see that his company gets paid for goods sold or services rendered. When one of his customers approaches insolvency and can't pay, it is often the credit man who sends the customer to a bankruptcy lawyer. The lawyer, of course, is grateful.

An out-of-court settlement case is initiated by the calling of a meeting of creditors. The minute a notice of a meeting goes out, or sometimes even before, the jockeying begins. Lawyers start calling up credit men, credit men start calling accountants, accountants call lawyers—all for the purpose of lining up votes.

By the time the meeting is held (usually within a few days after the notice goes out), everything is pretty well set up. It's very much like a political convention, in which the action on the floor is ritual while the real decisions are being made in the smoke-filled rooms.

The bankruptcy professionals operate with great subtlety, and the man whose business is in trouble hasn't the foggiest idea what's happening. He thinks that all these creditors are at the meeting to hear what his problems are and to see what can be done to help. Actually most of the professionals are there to stack the creditors' committee, get their favorites elected as committee counsel, committee accountant and committee secretary—the three fee-paying jobs that will emerge from the meeting. After the election is over, they lose all interest in the case and go on to the next one.

1 A Kipper Is Not a Herring

The loft is hot and dusty. A group of grizzled, middle-aged men in shirt sleeves and baggy pants stand in a cluster around another middle-aged man on a wooden milk crate. The scene resembles a political discussion in Union Square. It's a bankruptcy auction.

A business that goes into bankruptcy usually has some assets—inventory, machinery, real estate, accounts receivable. It's the function of the bankruptcy administration to turn these assets into cash to be distributed to creditors. In practice, the administrators turn the assets into cash mainly so they can pay their own fees.

There is a tight-knit group of auctioneers who specialize in the appraisal and sale of bankrupts' property. The buyers at these auctions, many of them auctioneers themselves, look as though they would have trouble finding two quarters to rub together. But they know their business and come with big bankrolls (only cash and certified checks are accepted), and heaven help the novice who comes in to bid against them.

Bankruptcy sales are conducted at lightning speed. An

experienced auctioneer knocks down a hundred lots an hour. That's almost two a minute, so it's easy to see there's not much time for vacillation. You've got to make instant decisions. The pros can do it. But it's no place for an amateur.

The consumer doesn't stand much of a chance to pick up any bargains at a bankruptcy auction. The entire operation is geared to the trade—that is, other auctioneers or dealers. Some of the promotional retailers like Filene's of Boston or Alexander's in New York send buyers to these sales looking for off-price merchandise.

A little dress shop went under in my neighborhood, and at the auction $7 sweaters were going at $2 each, and $10 retail sellers were knocked down at $2.50 apiece. That sounds like a pretty good buy, but if you wanted the $7 numbers, you had to buy twenty-five of them in assorted sizes and colors. You couldn't buy the $10 jobs separately either.

Aside from not being able to buy just the one piece you want, there's the matter of warranties. There's no such thing at a bankruptcy sale. If you buy something and it falls apart in your hands, that's tough.

There are no guarantees, no warranties, no representations of any kind. You can inspect the merchandise before the sale, but once the bidding starts, there's no time for quality control tests. Everything is sold where it is and as it is. There's no turning back. You pay cash and you get everything out by four in the afternoon and that's it.

Distress sales usually bring in between 30 and 70 percent of the wholesale price, depending on market conditions and the type of goods involved. Liquor will realize between 80 and 90 percent of original cost, and some branded perfumes and colognes might fetch dollar for dollar at auction. Some merchandise won't bring a tenth of cost.

Market conditions are important. At one time a particular brand of milling machine that wholesaled for $2,400 brand new would bring $2,800 secondhand at an auction because the machine was in short supply. A couple of years later an auctioneer was lucky to get $500 or $600 for the same type of machine.

One form of dirty pool at an auction is known as a kipper. The bidders get together before the sale, decide who will bid how much for what, and when it's over they get together again and work out their own deals. A sharp auctioneer can spot the fix, but the uninitiated can easily be sucked in. Kippers are not too well publicized, but occasionally the news slips out.

Bankruptcy and assignee's sales (an assignment for the benefit of creditors is a state court equivalent of the Federal bankruptcy procedure) are sometimes held in court with judges or referees serving as auctioneers. This will happen when there is an early bid for all the assets in a particular case. The court sends out notices advertising the upset price and hopes other bidders will show up to run the price up. If no one else bids at the hearing, the assets go for the upset price.

Bankruptcy referees or state court judges who have had experience in insolvency cases and know the score can spot a kipper. They'll either get the bidders competing against each other or they just won't approve the sale.

But some years back a state court judge was completely taken in. A store was being auctioned off, and one of the professionals had put in a $20,000 bid for the whole place.

A notice went out asking creditors or any other interested parties to show cause why the sale shouldn't be approved for the $20,000 or any higher bid, and a hearing was held.

On the date of the hearing the courtroom was packed. The terms of the sale were read off with the $20,000 upset price, and the judge called for other bids.

Dead silence.

He called again. Still no bids. He began asking questions. What are all you people doing here? Nothing.

Finally, in utter exasperation, the judge knocked down the assets to the original bidder for $20,000. About a week later the successful bidder held an auction of his own, and the same stuff brought $32,000. Furthermore, a number of auctioneers in court on the day of the kipper got $100 checks for their cooperation.

The plot leaked out in credit circles when one of the $100 checks found its way into the hands of a suspicious credit man, and the incident sparked a noisy but largely ineffectual campaign to "clean up the adjustment business."

Creditors were incensed because they got $20,000 for $32,000 worth of their assets. The business is no cleaner or dirtier today than it was before the great kipper.

Secrecy carried to the extreme is characteristic of the bankruptcy auction. Nobody except the auctioneer knows who is bidding what, and sometimes even he doesn't know whom the bidder really represents. Lawyers bid without disclosing the clients they're bidding for. The bidder could be a representative of the bankrupt, buying back his own merchandise cheaply; dealers representing other dealers' bids; auctioneers representing groups. It's all calculated to confuse.

The rationale behind some of the secrecy, aside from a bankrupt not wanting anyone to know he's buying back his business, is to keep the competition off guard.

If a dealer has a reputation for being a shrewd operator, other less knowledgeable buyers might try riding on the shrewd one's back.

If Sam the astute is willing to bid $150 for a machine, it must be worth much more than that, so I can't go wrong bidding $160, goes the thinking. This is a dangerous game because Sam can lead you up the daisy path if he thinks you're trying to cash in on his expertise. He'll just bid up a piece of junk and then stick you with it. The whole business is a big poker game.

To confuse the follow-the-leader types, the smart and/or suspicious bidders use signals that they set up in advance with the auctioneer. One old-timer used a cigarette. As long as he kept the cigarette in his mouth, he was bidding. When he had gone as high as he intended, he'd just remove the cigarette. Some bidders lift their hands or touch their elbows or wink or nod. Be careful what you do at a bankruptcy sale. You might just scratch your nose and find yourself the owner of fifteen cases of Christmas wrap.

Most bankruptcy sales are reasonably honest, but there are some sharp practices, and the professionals have the edge over the auction buff who may have had his training on the boardwalk of Atlantic City.

When an auctioneer is assigned the job of selling a bankrupt's property, there is an appraisal made and the merchandise is sorted into lots. A buyer with friends on the auctioneer's staff could learn that a certain lot that looks like garbage has hidden value.

"We had a bunch of clocks in a barrel to sell," said one

insider, "and we put the cheap ones on the top and some very expensive ones way down on the bottom. One of the buyers was tipped off. He went higher than the rest because he knew something that they didn't."

In selling fabrics it is easy to fake the yardage. A bolt of cloth with 250 yards can be marked 200 yards and this intelligence leaked to a favored buyer. All merchandise is open to inspection before the sale, but who is going to take the time to measure the yardage on a bolt of cloth?

The buyer who knows he's getting an extra full measure can bid more per yard than the competition who is relying on the yardage as represented.

With no guarantees a buyer at a bankruptcy sale is rolling the dice. He'll get stuck sometimes, but he hopes to make it up the next time with an extra good buy.

One pro tells of a radio-TV repairman who, with his special knowledge, doubled as an appraiser in appliance-store bankruptcies.

"Whenever he went out on an appraisal job, he carried this huge suitcase with him. Nobody could figure out why the hell he'd drag this dumb satchel around with him wherever he went. We thought it may have been some kind of testing equipment. It turned out to be full of old burned-out tubes which he'd use to replace the new ones in the inventory he was appraising."

There are lots of stories of hanky-panky at auctions. There's the case of this landlord who had lined up a good new tenant for his store that had just been vacated by a bankrupt. The fixtures were still in, and the landlord wanted to make sure they'd stay because the new tenant wanted them.

He went to the trustee and made a deal to buy the

fixtures for $5,000. All the landlord had to do was show up at the auction and there would be no problem about being the successful bidder.

When the bidding on the fixtures started, there was competition. One particularly stubborn bidder stayed with the landlord's bid all the way.

When the price reached $3,500, the auctioneer conveniently called a recess, and the landlord's lawyer was approached by his major competitor.

"Hey," he said, "do you really want this stuff?"

"Yes," the lawyer admitted.

"O.K., give me a thousand dollars and it's yours."

The lawyer agreed, and that did it. When the recess was over, the auctioneer came back with the announcement, "The fixtures being sold are subject to a landlord's claim. Any buyer does so at his peril."

That chilled the bidding, and the landlord got his fixtures for $3,500—plus $1,000 to his enterprising opponent and another $1,500 to bring the trustee's take to the $5,000 agreed upon.

Among the abuses at auctions is the fast knockdown. If an auctioneer wants to see that a friendly buyer gets a break, he can just mumble a few numbers and, before anyone knows what's happening, give his buddy a particular plum. The auctioneer can get away with this gambit once in a while, but the smart buyers won't sit still very long.

And buyers have their own little tricks. They renege on bids or try to chisel the auctioneer down.

They'll say they bid only $250 for a lot when the auctioneer has it down for $500. Or they can deny ever bidding at all for a particular lot.

If the auctioneer complains, the buyer can threaten to take it up with the license commission. In New York City, as in most other areas, auctioneers are licensed, and if they lose their license they're out of business.

Then there's always the kipper. Larry F. Hecht of David Strauss & Company has been running bankruptcy sales for twenty-five years and says that every sale is a kipper.

"When you've been in the business awhile," he says, "you can smell them. If you see five people in the crowd who can use the same piece of equipment and they aren't bidding, you know something is up.

"We know what everything should bring, and if the bidders won't give us a realistic bid, we push them. We'll bid ourselves. We're not interested in buying at our own auctions, but we bid if the price seems out of line. So far we've been lucky and haven't had to buy very much.

"You might have ten buyers all in a combination against the auctioneer, and if you know your business, before long they'll be bidding against each other and you'll have a real auction going.

"You must know the value of the merchandise you're selling. Also I think we have a sixth sense. Look into a man's eyes and you can tell if he really wants a particular item. The eyes give him away, and then it's up to you to induce him to bid."

Auctioneers are paid a percentage of the gross, so it's to their interest to get the best price for everything they sell. In bankruptcy sales the auctioneer gets 7½ percent of the first $10,000, 5 percent of the next $5,000 and 3 percent after that. This formula varies somewhat from district to district. In the Eastern District of New York, which takes in Brooklyn and Long Island, the auctioneer's commission is 6 percent of the first $5,000 and 3 percent of the balance. In assignment cases, the auctioneer gets a flat 7 percent.

In addition to insolvency sales, a firm like David Strauss handles sheriff sales, foreclosures, finance-company sales and private jobs. Where there is no fee set by the court, the fee is negotiated. Hecht says he shoots for 10 percent but might go down to 7 percent if circumstances warrant.

As I mentioned earlier, assignments are administered in state court, while bankruptcy is under the Federal court jurisdiction. There are other differences.

Assignments generally are used in the smaller cases, those in which the creditors don't have enough of a stake to make a Federal case over.

An assignment can provide the vehicle for a quick liquidation with less red tape than bankruptcy. The New York Credit Men's Adjustment Bureau, a nonprofit group representing creditor interest, will often liquidate a case under an assignment and then bring it over to the bankruptcy courts if creditors think an extensive investigation is required.

When a case is pushed into bankruptcy from an assignment proceeding, the auctioneer may also get a shafting. In the Southern District of New York (Manhattan, the Bronx and several upstate counties), Underwriters Salvage Company is the official auctioneer for all bankruptcy sales.

An assignment is often a friendly arrangement under which a financially ailing businessman turns over all his assets to his own attorney, who becomes assignee. The lawyer then picks someone to be attorney to the assignee (usually the assignee's law partner), and they have a party. The assignee gets a commission and his partner gets a fee. Most organized creditor groups frown on this procedure, and if there's enough money involved, the creditors will do their best to force the debtor's attorney to resign as assignee and substitute the creditors' nominee. If the assignee won't go along, the creditors can throw the whole case into bankruptcy, where the creditors can elect their representative as trustee.

Dividends to general creditors as the result of liquidations in assignment proceedings, while not unheard of, are rare. There was a time when one of our trade papers used stories of closed-out assignments as fillers. Almost all of them started the same way: "Creditors of Blatz Company, which assigned, will receive no dividend . . ." These items became known around the office as "creditors get nuttin" stories.

If an auctioneer is selected in the assignment proceeding and the case goes over to bankruptcy before the sale is held, the original auctioneer gets kicked out. He gets paid only his out-of-pocket expenses for lotting, advertising or whatever else was done in preparing for the aborted sale.

"It's unfair," says Hecht. "We have to file all kinds of legal papers just to get back our expenses, and 99.9 percent of the time we have to wait for our money."

Appraisals are an integral part of the auctioneering business, but this doesn't usually involve big money. An auctioneer may get $50 or $100 for an appraisal, but Hecht says, "We never turn any down. We do it for the good will."

As a safeguard against crooked sales an independent appraisal is made before every bankruptcy sale. The appraisal is kept confidential until after the sale is completed. At least 75 percent of the appraised value must be realized or the sale will not be approved by the court except by special hearing. Hecht says that in all the years he's been in the business, he's never had a sale that brought less than 75 percent of the appraisal.

One of the games played at a bankruptcy auction is beat-the-bulk-bid. At the opening of every sale, after the auctioneer rattles off the terms and tells everyone that they have to put down 25 percent in cash on every bid and get the rest up in cash or certified check within twenty-four hours and how they have to take the stuff out as it stands, there is a call for a bulk bid. That is, a single price for the whole deal. After the bulk bidding is over, the small-lot bidding starts.

At the end of the sale, the small-lot bids are totaled, and if they top the bulk bid, the small-lot bidders get to take home their bargains. If the bulk bid is higher, everyone says, "Aw, shit" and goes up to get his deposit back.

As the small-lot sale progresses, the running total is kept secret to avoid any distortion in the bidding. If, for example, the bulk bid was $50,000, the small-lotters have bid a total of $49,900, and there's just one more lot to go—a batch of paper clips worth maybe $10. A small-lot bidder who thinks he's made some good buys during the sale could bid $110 for the $10 lot just to carry the total over the top. He might even get some of his co-bidders to pick up part of the extra-generous bid.

As a practical matter, it's impossible to keep the running total secret.

The buyers are a sharp bunch. They have pencils and pads, and at any point in the sale they can tell you to the penny how much has been bid up to that time.

It's a frustrating experience to go through the agony of bidding, winning some, losing some, and then ending up empty-handed when the bulk bidder carries the day. A large sale I covered some years back lasted for three days, with crowds of eager bidders pushing and shoving their way around a dreary factory and warehouse and the auctioneers working in shifts and chanting themselves hoarse. When it was over, the small-lotters were nowhere near the $1.5 million that a finance company with a mortgage on all the assets had bid. As it turned out, the finance company had a buyer ready to pay $1.6 million for the property.

As for the small-lot bidders, all they had to show for three days' hard work was sore feet and a ringing in their ears.

Auctioneers are not much for show or fancy trimmings. David Strauss occupies a dinky store front on West 29th Street in Manhattan and looks like a prime candidate for Federal anti-poverty aid.

There's some off-price clothing on plain pipe racks and wooden counters on the street floor and a couple of simple functional offices one flight up.

David Strauss & Company is one of the biggest auction firms in New York City. Arthur Albert & Company, which gets all the work from the New York Credit Men's Adjustment Bureau, and Underwriters Salvage are two other majors in town. The Strauss firm handles about 300 sales a year and does a multimillion-dollar gross. It gets business from the top bankruptcy lawyers, from finance companies and from the courts. Strauss also has a lock on the distress sales in the ever-distressed New York fur market.

Auctioneering is a rough business. In one working day an auctioneer might sell about 1,000 lots. Sales rarely are interrupted for lunch. Sometimes, if a sale is going well and the auctioneer stands to make a good pay day, he'll spring for sandwiches. But the bidding goes on between bites.

As to the honesty or lack thereof in the business—all you can get are rumors.

"We hear all these stories," says one bankruptcy lawyer, "but I don't know how many are true. Yet if everything is on the up and up, how come an auctioneer had a piano delivered to a credit man I know?"

2 Cheaper than Wholesale

There's the story in the garment business about a retailer who constantly advertised that he sold his merchandise "below wholesale" and swore that the ads were true.

He was about to hire a new accountant, and the cost-conscious auditor wanted to get a few points clarified.

"Before I take on this assignment," the accountant said, "we've got to get one thing straight. This business of selling below wholesale has just got to stop."

"I can't," said the entrepreneur. "My whole business is based on the policy of selling below wholesale."

"But," said the accountant, "how the hell do you expect to make any money with that kind of policy?"

"I can sell below wholesale," he explained simply, "because I buy below wholesale."

All of which leads to a true story of a mink coat manufacturer—we'll call him Joe Green—who set the fur market on its ear back in 1950. Within about a year and a half he became one of the biggest in the business. He grew so rapidly because he sold his coats at a price lower than anyone else in the market.

As he grew, his suppliers extended him larger and larger credits. One of the more sophisticated creditors, nervous over his large exposure, grew suspicious because the manufacturer's prices seemed out of line. Having such a large stake in Green's business, the creditor thought he had a right to look at the books to satisfy himself that everything was as warranted.

But Joe would have none of it. "I have a secret production method," he said, "and I can't let anybody find out about it."

Not too long afterward Joe went broke, and the secret of his price-cutting came out: Joe wasn't paying for all his skins.

He'd been buying skins in large quantities, taking a portion of his purchase to the neighborhood loan shark, where he'd pledge the skins at 50 cents on the dollar. He'd use the cash to pay some of his bills, then order still more, which he'd hock on the same terms. The laws of geometric progression being what they are, Mr. Green quickly reached the point where he could no longer support the pyramid, and down it all tumbled. A colorful, charming and, in his own mind, well-intentioned individual, Green was angry at his creditors for pressing him for money. And right up to the day they sent him off to jail he insisted, "If they had just given me a little more time, they all would have been paid off."

The ingenuity of the bankruptcy swindler is a never ending source of wonder and grudging admiration. Whenever the credit men think they've seen it all, somebody comes up with a new wrinkle.

One recent fraud involved a scheme to siphon off thousands of dollars' worth of merchandise from a textile company by exporting to a phantom foreign customer. The management of the American company knew they were in trouble and about to go under, so they decided to set a little aside as a stake for a new venture.

All the company records showed were some perfectly legitimate-looking sales to a customer in Europe. The customer apparently had his own financial troubles and couldn't pay for the goods. Now this is not unusual in the textile business, so it looked like a normal bad debt.

But looking deeper into the transactions, the creditors learned that the European company and the American seller were working together. The importer was selling the goods off-price for cash and, after taking his cut, sending back the cash to the owners of the American company.

John C. Fredell Jr., who heads the Fraud Prevention division of the New York Credit and Financial Management Association, has spent twenty years investigating bankruptcy frauds. He divides crooked bankrupts into two categories—those who go into business specifically to steal from creditors and those who turn to fraud in the hope of saving their businesses and eventually paying their debts.

The latter are usually the most painful to creditors. "The well-intentioned fraud can do more harm to his creditors than the out-and-out crook," Fredell says.

The normal mode of operation for the credit thief is to spread his business around, ordering small quantities of merchandise from a large number of suppliers. While in the aggregate he may run up a sizable debt, no single creditor is hurt too badly. "But," says Fredell, "the established businessman can place large orders with a limited number of suppliers, and when he goes under he can take some of his creditors with him.

Unfortunately, adversity can bring out the little larceny in all of us. It's easy to be ethical if everything is going well. There's no need to steal. But if business is rotten and the bill collectors are constantly breathing down your back, the temptation to cheat can be overwhelming. Phony fires and burglaries are among the more popular ploys, as illustrated by the stories the boys in the bankruptcy business tell each other.

There's the one about the two manufacturers who meet at a plush hotel in Miami Beach and begin to discuss their respective businesses.

"I'm down here," volunteers the first manufacturer, "taking it easy while my plant is being rebuilt. I had a terrible fire, and the insurance company is building me a whole new factory."

"That's a coincidence," says the second manufacturer. "I had a flood in my plant and everything was ruined. Now the insurance company is building me a brand-new modern showplace. That flood was the best thing that ever happened to me."

The first manufacturer looks impressed, draws closer to his companion and in a confidential tone whispers, "Tell me, how do you make a flood?"

And a quickie about burglaries. Again we find two shifty types who meet in the street, exchange pleasantries and one says, "Ed, I hear you had a robbery at your place last week."

"Not last week, stupid, next week," snaps Ed.

While most hard-pressed businessmen avoid the extremes of setting up fake robberies or turning to arson, corner-cutting under the pressure of faltering finances is not uncommon.

You may try selling some of your inventory below cost to get cash to pay your most insistent creditors; you may dress up your financial statement with a few white lies, always assuming that business will get better and everything will be paid and the question of the financial statement just won't come up. However, if things keep going downhill and you have to call your creditors together, those little liberties look like FRAUD to irritated, unpaid suppliers.

Insolvencies in which "irregularities" are found can be approached by creditors in three ways. They can just overlook the ethical deficiencies and take a quick settlement; they can insist that because there has been dishonesty they won't negotiate and will make every effort to force a prosecution; or the creditors can insist on a settlement larger than the figures would call for if the case were honest.

That is, creditors in a sense assess damages against the debtor for his transgressions.

In blatant frauds there's no problem—they try to get a prosecution. But the borderline cases in which reasonably honest men make reasonably dishonest decisions to save their business skins are the stickiest to handle.

A case comes to mind of a manufacturer who issued a false financial statement—the manufacturer's lawyer claimed that his client meant well but was misled by an accountant. The business deteriorated and a creditors' meeting had to be convened. During negotiations creditors were offered 50 percent of their claims, considerably more than could be expected in bankruptcy.

The debtor's attorney argued that a 50 percent settlement would involve some painful sacrifices on the part of his client. The errant manufacturer would have to borrow to the hilt to make the settlement and sweat for years to pay the money back.

A majority of the creditors' committee agreed to go along, but the dissenters were insistent enough to kill the deal.

The argument used was the old foot-in-the-door bit. "If we let this one get away with it, we'll have everyone in the country sending us phony statements."

It was decided to throw the company into bankruptcy, hold an investigation and turn over the results to the United States attorney in the hope of a prosecution.

Under the best of circumstances, justice takes time, and in bankruptcy cases the wheels hardly turn at all. While the lawyers and accountants busied themselves rounding up evidence, the principal of the bankrupt set up shop again. During the five years between the bankruptcy and the indictment, he had developed a swinging business, and most of the creditors who had been stuck in the last case were again extending large amounts of credit to the new business.

When sentencing day arrived the creditors were faced with a dilemma. If they were to continue to seek retribution for past sins and ask for a jail term, they would have to take another bath. With the brains of the business in jail, they knew they wouldn't get paid on the new debt.

A practical approach was taken. The court suspended sentence, and the last time I looked the business was growing rapidly, the issuer of the phony statement was a millionaire and suppliers were knocking each other down to get new orders.

As a general rule, prosecuting attorneys are reluctant to

take bankruptcy fraud cases because there's rarely any publicity in it for them. They prefer the crime-syndicate cases that get splashed over the front pages. Government people also contend that many so-called bankruptcy fraud cases are just creditors' efforts to use the prosecutor as a collection agency for unpaid debts. If creditors come in with an airtight case, they might get a prosecutor to take it on, but otherwise it's don't call us, we'll call you.

The most spectacular fraud to hit Philadelphia in the last decade started out as a bankruptcy case that was initially turned down by the United States attorney's office in Philadelphia.

The central character was Sylvan Scolnick, better known as Cherry Hill Fats, a con man weighing over 600 pounds who in the late 1950s and early '60s seemed to have had his pudgy fingers in just about every shady operation within fifty miles of Philadelphia.

His many-faceted exploits in themselves would have been enough to keep the most eager of crime reporters busy day and night. But Scolnick added an extra dimension to the story—his monumental size. He had a 152-inch waist, 136-inch chest, 168-inch hips and wore size 19 shoes.

He was so big that he had to be wheeled in and out of the courtroom on a park bench, perched atop a post-office freight dolly.

He ate as much as five average men.

In Lewisburg, the Federal prison where he served time for bankruptcy fraud, he had to have two beds strapped together for him and nine meals a day; he had to have a ground-floor cell so he wouldn't have to climb steps; it took three tailors to sew up a prison uniform that would fit him.

The headline writers in Philadelphia had a ball: "642 Pounder Ruled Fat but Fit"; "Scolnick Cuts Down to 9 Meals a Day"; and "Scolnick Drops Role of a 'Heavy,' Gets Off Lightly."

In July of 1964 Scolnick broke into the Philadelphia papers when he showed up as a witness before a grand jury investigating a possible bankruptcy fraud involving M. Stein & Company, a general merchandise firm headed by Scolnick's father-in-law. The company went broke in 1959 after having bought about $1 million worth of merchandise over an eight-month period.

Scolnick was indicted for bankruptcy fraud in the Stein case about seven months later. The indictment said that from January to December of 1959 there was a conspiracy to buy merchandise on credit, not to pay for it, to keep the business going as long as possible and then to go bankrupt and conceal the proceeds of the merchandise from the bankruptcy trustee.

The indictment charged concealment of $603,665.17, and the wide variety of goods followed the time-honored pattern of the scam operation. Merchandise ranged from bicycles and radios to cookies and Easter eggs.

The indictment opened a can of phony bankruptcy worms that ultimately resulted in sixteen indictments and broke the back of a large bankruptcy ring operating in the Philadelphia area.

Scolnick tried to delay his trial, contending that because of his weight his heart couldn't stand the strain. He asked for time to lose weight and at one point had an electrocardiogram taken right in the courtroom. But the court ruled that he would have to stand trial and when it was about to start he entered a guilty plea.

In October of 1966 he was sentenced to five years and went off to Lewisburg Federal Prison. While the prison authorities were busying themselves trying to adjust to their mountainous inmate, other stories of Scolnick's colorful past began to surface.

A fire in March of 1965 destroyed seven buildings in Philadelphia. It had started in the offices of Regency Builders, Inc. Our fat friend, Sylvan Scolnick, turned up as promotion head and part owner of Regency. He admitted paying $4,000 to have the fire set. When the flames died down, the damage to seven buildings added up to $643,000, the largest man-made fire in Philadelphia's history.

The payoff for the Regency fire was supposed to have gone to one Sidney Brooks, a Scolnick colleague dubbed the "master burglar" by the Philadelphia newspapers.

Brooks apparently earned this appellation by breaking into his own safety-deposit box and stealing $100,000 of his own money. It seemed the money was under a Federal seal placed by the Internal Revenue Service. Scolnick worked out the plan to break in and steal it and then sue the Government and/or the bank for allowing the money to be stolen. But the job was bungled, and Brooks and two accomplices were arrested.

A Philadelphia detective charged with extortion was also mixed up with Scolnick. The detective shook Scolnick down for $5,000 in exchange for silence about some of the Big Man's activities. The detective also agreed to keep Scolnick posted on evidence the police turned up against him.

On top of this, the super thief was linked to another shakedown case involving a Philadelphia newsman.

In the end, Scolnick became a veritable fountain of information on the Philadelphia underworld. He spent 1,200 hours spilling his ample guts to the Philadelphia district attorney, and the DA said the testimony threw light on a wide assortment of crimes, including a hijacking, a diamond theft and a $2 million counterfeiting ring. His information additionally resulted in the recovery of $200,000 worth of stolen goods.

When in March of 1968 Scolnick came up for sentencing in connection with the Brooks safety-deposit-box gambit, the DA pleaded for clemency, and Scolnick was all remorse. Scolnick got off without any time added to his five-year bankruptcy-fraud sentence.

The Philadelphia *Inquirer,* in its issue of March 30, 1968, described the scene:

A contrite Sylvan Scolnick listened to eulogies of his reformed self on Friday, then with an angelic smile on his fat face, told a U.S. District Court Judge he knew now what he did during his life-long career of crime.

"I didn't realize so much was involved until you hear it all at one time," the 500-pound bankruptcy fraud expert from Cherry Hill, N.J. told Judge A. Leon Higginbotham, Jr.

"I guess, Judge, I was on a merry-go-round and didn't realize what was happening.

"But since I've been in jail, for the first time I had a chance to realize what I did to myself, my family and the people that have been good to me.

"I feel that by doing what I've done—by helping these different [law enforcement] agencies—I may have offset some of the harm that I have done."

Scolnick has since completed his term at Lewisburg— he was paroled in May of 1970—and actually spent little time in prison. He was always busy testifying at trials, talking to the Federal Bureau of Investigation or the Philadelphia district attorney.

He came out of jail a new man, telling reporters that he felt like a "newborn baby." Little more than a year later, the October 1971 issue of *Philadelphia Magazine* published a detailed investigative report of Scolnick's latest caper—an advertising hustle involving the sale of local publishing rights to a book offering consumers up to $1,500 in discounts for $10.

The major requirements for a successful phony bankruptcy are charm and big balls, and Scolnick had more than his share of both. He could sell anybody anything, and before the bottom dropped out he even managed to con the FBI.

About five years before the bankruptcy-fraud indictment creditor sources were advised that after a thorough investigation by the FBI of the 1959 M. Stein & Company bankruptcy, the U.S. attorney in Philadelphia had decided to close the case because he was unable to establish a foundation for a prosecution.

Despite the Sylvan Scolnicks there's an overall impression among credit grantors that crooked bankruptcies are not nearly so prevalent as they were back in the Depression days of the 1930s. This impression is disputed by Harry A. Margolis, an attorney who was active in the Thirties doing investigative work for creditors and who still looks at every bankruptcy he handles with a professionally jaundiced eye.

"There are as many phony bankruptcies today as there were in the Twenties and Thirties," says Margolis, who looks like what you would get if you crossed a lion with a bulldog and sent it to law school.

"Human nature never changes. Only the names and faces are different. Guys in business will try to clip you just like they did in the early days. They're just a little more sophisticated today. The crooks are better and the guys who are charged with the job of ferreting them out aren't as dedicated."

But the old days did have their share of colorful capers.

Margolis recalls the old Bond Dress Company case, which made a bankruptcy splash in the early 1930s. This was one of the biggest firms in the field and had the added attraction of a big show-business name of the day—Helen Kane, the Boop-Boop-a-Doop girl.

Helen let one of the partners in Bond Dress handle her money. She was earning $5,000 a week, an astronomical sum for that era, and he took it all, gave her an allowance and invested the rest in Bond Dress.

In all about $165,000 went into the business as loans from Miss Kane. Then business at Bond began to fall off, and the singer, who was much sharper than her Boop-Boop-a-Doop image, wanted out. So Bond made a huge sale of inventory for cash (cash sales are a favorite method of siphoning money out of a business) and repaid Miss Kane her $165,000.

Bond went broke less than four months later, and the trustee attacked the $165,000 payment as a preference and sued to get it back. Under bankruptcy law, if one creditor gets a larger share of his debt than the rest of the creditors in the same class within four months of a bankruptcy, that payment is preferential and can be recovered for the estate.

It's one thing to sue for money and another to get it. Miss Kane had deposited the $165,000 in a safety-deposit box in Chicago under an assumed name, and after much investigation the money was located and tied up. A settlement was finally worked out. Miss Kane got to keep about $60,000, and the rest went into the Bond Dress estate for creditors.

Bankruptcy is a decidedly unpleasant experience, and most businessmen regard it as unthinkable. But there are those who try to make a good thing out of phony bankruptcies and such related activities as faked burglaries.

One classic staged robbery involved two partners in a fur business back in the 1950s. One partner loaded up his car with furs in preparation for a sales trip. He took off and that night called his partner from Philadelphia in a state of hysteria.

"Jack, I've been held up. Two guys jumped in my car. They took my watch and all my money and then drove off with the car. Almost our whole inventory was in the car. What should I do?"

"Go to the police and report it and then come back. We'll do the best we can."

In view of the loss of inventory, the partners called their creditors together, explained their misfortune and asked for a settlement. The creditors wanted 60 percent but were offered only 50, and the negotiations fell apart over the 10 percent difference. The case went into bankruptcy.

Meanwhile, the partners filed an insurance claim for the car (the furs weren't covered but the car was), and that was their undoing.

An investigator for the insurance company found the car in a junkyard in the Bronx and began asking questions.

Here's the story that emerged:

Instead of driving to Philadelphia, the furrier drove out to a relative's place on Long Island and put the furs in a freezer. He turned the car over to a friend for disposal and took a train to Philadelphia. There he went to the nearest police station, told them about this terrible robbery and called his partner. The phone call was just for the record, because both were in on the plot.

Before the case was over, each was blaming the other for the whole deal, and both were kicking themselves for not paying creditors that extra 10 percent and for greedily trying to get the few bucks from the insurance company for the car.

Attorney Margolis tells of a bankrupt who got away with several well-timed burglaries in the Thirties but who went to jail twenty-five years later on a concealment charge. Mr. Margolis, representing the trustee in the two bankruptcies involved, couldn't prove that the burglaries were planned, but he got lucky in the concealment case.

As Mr. Margolis recalls it, the bankruptcy pro—we'll call him Jack Glass—was in the millinery business and was burglarized with great regularity. The first burglary was covered by insurance, and the underwriter paid without question. The second burglary was questioned by the insurance company, which paid reluctantly. But the insurer refused to issue any further policies, so the next robbery had to come out of the creditors' hides.

It came and followed the pattern of the rest. There was a hole cut in the ceiling through which the burglars were supposed to have pulled the hat bodies and made off with them from the loft above. The hole was twenty inches wide. The hat bodies were twenty-two inches wide. The locks in the loft above were apparently broken from the inside. The hole in the ceiling had ragged edges, but there were no signs of fibers caught around the rim. It all looked mighty suspicious.

The trustee reasoned that the hat bodies were taken out the front door, loaded in a truck and sold for cash. The hole in the ceiling and the broken locks were designed to cover over the cash sales.

The issue came to trial and the robbery stood up, largely on the basis of testimony by a detective who was rumored to have been bribed to testify that a legitimate burglary had taken place.

More than twenty years later this same Jack Glass turned up as the principal in another bankruptcy with an odor to it.

In this case there were some suspicious checks that couldn't be traced out. The checks were made out to companies that couldn't be located. It was apparent that the checks were used to draw money out of the business.

But proving this was another matter. The break in the case came in the form of a $300 check paid to a hotel in Miami Beach, signed by one Steven Shram (that's not his real name) as a vice-president of Glass's company. There was no one named Shram on Glass's payroll. Mr. Shram was a bad-check artist who, at the time of the bankruptcy, was in Sing Sing Prison serving time for his propensity to draw against nonexistent funds.

Mr. Margolis went up to visit Shram in Sing Sing to see what he could learn.

Shram said he had known Glass for years and had some friends who had made up phony invoices and cashed checks for Glass's companies. Shram gave every indication of being a prime source. But before telling some strange lawyer everything, he wanted to make a deal.

"What do I get out of this?" Shram asked.

"What did you have in mind?" Margolis countered.

"Five thousand dollars."

"Forget it. Your information isn't worth five hundred dollars. Furthermore, if I tell the Florida police about that three-hundred-dollar check, they'll pick you up and throw you back in the can as soon as you get out of this place. But I suppose I could dig up five hundred."

With that, Margolis got up to leave, but Shram wasn't finished.

"Hold it. I know a lot about Glass. How about twenty-five hundred?"

"I'll check it out and see what I can do," the lawyer said, and he left.

As Margolis tells it: "I went back to New York and called the major creditors together. The guys I could trust.

"I told them about the meeting with Shram and told them that money for this kind of payoff couldn't come out of the estate. They would each have to make a donation to an 'investigation fund.' They got up sixteen hundred dollars that I put into a special account.

"I went up to see him again and told him, 'Fifteen hundred is yours. Take it or leave it.' I needed the extra hundred for incidentals, and he agreed to the fifteen hundred dollars. The next question was how to give him the money. I wasn't going to give it to him right away. I was going to dole it out a little at a time. 'Talk first and when I get the information, you get the money.'

"Before going ahead with the deal Shram wanted to give me a test. It was his girl friend's birthday and he told me to buy her flowers and candy and give her twenty-five dollars. It came to about forty-five dollars altogether. I was also supposed to tell her to write him that I'd been there and had followed his instructions.

"I went up to see her—she was a real looker too—told her I was a friend of Steven Shram, wished her a happy birthday, gave her the flowers and everything else Steven wanted her to have. I passed the first test.

"But he wanted to test me again. He wanted me to bring another twenty-five dollars to his mother in a greeting card he signed. I brought it and the poor old lady had tears in her eyes.

"I passed the tests, gave him another twenty-five dollars that he said he needed and then we'd send up twenty-five dollars every couple of weeks and he was happy.

"I brought up a stenographer and he told us all about the cash sales, the phony entries and the phony invoices. That formed the basis for a concealment case against Glass. A jury took forty minutes to find him guilty, and he got two years.

"Sometimes it takes a thief to catch a thief."

3 Ten Cents on the Dollar, or Reading Between the Lies

A meeting of creditors is like old home week. Everyone seems to know everyone else and there is much shaking of hands and slapping of backs and general good fellowship. It's something like the funeral of a lady who died at ninety-five after a full life and who left a great fortune to be divided up among the surviving relatives.

After all the "hellos" and "how are yous" and the "good to see yous," the ubiquitous question is, "How much are you in for?"

"I'm stuck for ten thousand dollars and this was my first order from the sonofabitch. I called him just last week and he promised to put a check in the mail. That bastard knew he was busted all the time."

"I figured he ran a crappy outfit from the beginning, but I had this piece goods I couldn't unload anywhere else, so I shipped it to him. I even sent him more than he ordered, so what the hell. If I get ten cents on the dollar, I'm still ahead."

"Hey, who you gonna vote for in this case? I got a call from Harry this morning. He wants this one. Listen, you

vote for Harry and next meeting you got my vote. O.K.?
This is no great shakes, but there should be enough there
for a fee. Harry says I screwed him on the last one—no
assets. Just a lot of work. So let's see if we can get this for
him." So goes the conversation before the meeting starts,
with everyone feeling out everyone else to see how the
case shapes up fees-wise.

The format of a creditors' meeting is standardized. The
attorney for the strapped company will give the figures
and say a few kind words about how honest, hard-working
and deserving of consideration his client is. The client
may have been stealing the company blind and spending
most of his time gambling and cheating on his wife, but it
is incumbent upon the attorney to project a sympathetic
image for the client.

After the presentation is over, the creditors ask that the
debtor and his attorney leave the room—ostensibly because they want to discuss the company's affairs in private, but actually because they don't want the embarrass-
ment of the debtor watching them squabble among
themselves over the business of electing a committee.

Creditors and lawyers representing or purporting to
represent creditors begin making speeches about the
makeup of the committee.

"I think we should elect a committee of seventeen
members," says a lawyer from the back. This means the
learned counselor has a deal with several small creditors
and the only chance he has of getting the case or even
getting a piece of it is to have a large committee.

"I disagree," says a credit man from another part of the
room. "A seventeen-member committee would be entirely
too unwieldy to get anything accomplished. I recom-

mend a five-man committee made up of the largest creditors." This means the credit man has a large claim himself
or is friendly with a couple of large creditors who want to
control the committee, get their men to run the case and
control the fees.

"Small creditors have as much interest in this case as
the larger ones," says the first lawyer. "My client's two-
hundred-dollar claim means as much to him as your fifty
thousand." This means, "If you're so smart, how come you
got stuck so bad?"

The standard reply to the small creditor's bit is "The
interests of large creditors are the same as the small
creditor, and you can be sure that since they have such a
large stake in the case, they'll vigorously protect the
interests of all creditors." This means, "Shut up, you
sonofabitch. I know what you're up to and you're not
going to get away with it."

Another tactic used to keep small creditors from exer-
cising an inordinate influence in choosing the committee's
paid professionals is to try to con them into serving
without a vote.

One professional attender of creditors' meetings has
had particular success in mousetrapping the less knowledgeable credit men into complete impotence.

He'd wait until the meeting seemed to be getting out of
hand with everyone hollering about points of order and
amending motions and amending amendments to motions,
and he'd stand up and with a deep, resonant voice that
sounded as though it came down from the mountain, he'd
say, "Gentlemen, gentlemen. I think I have the solution. You
smaller creditors who want to serve on the committee—
why not serve as ex-officio members? You'll be notified of

all committee meetings, you'll have an opportunity to contribute your expertise to the solution of the debtor's problems, you'll participate in the negotiations and function in every way as a committee member." He would then add, with as little emphasis as possible, that the ex-officio members have no vote.

To the creditors who knew the score, a committee member without a vote is like a eunuch in a bordello—he might learn a lot, but it won't do him any good. But to the wide-eyed innocent who thought that the purpose of the creditors' committee was to get the best possible deal for creditors, ex-officio service made a lot of sense and some would fall for it.

The politicking involved in organizing a committee can go on for hours or it can be wound up in a few minutes, depending on how well organized the meeting was beforehand and how the balance of power shapes up. If one group has overwhelming strength, the matter of selecting the committee can be handled quickly. If there are several factions, each fairly evenly balanced, the election can take all day. The stakes involved also influence the energy thrown into elections. The bigger the case, the bigger the fee and the more vigorous the contest. A case involving several million dollars will inspire a much livelier meeting than a run-of-the-mill $50,000 bust.

Retail cases usually make for the most exciting meetings because retailers buy from so many different suppliers. A large retailer can have thousands of creditors, while a manufacturer can build up a mountainous debt with just a handful of creditors. The more creditors, the more factions, the more heated the contest.

The tightly contested cases involve much speechmak-

ing and parliamentary procedure and some tortured inter-
pretations of Robert's Rules of Order. Occasionally a well-
organized group of small creditors and noisy lawyers can
steal a case, but mostly the creditors stuck for the most
money get the privilege of calling the shots when it
comes to picking the attorneys, the accountants and the
committee secretary.

Once the committee is elected, the creditors' meeting is
adjourned, and the rest of the creditors are sent home to
await a report.

The first order of business for the committee is the
selection of the staff, and this is taken care of immediately
after the general meeting breaks up. Committee members
themselves get no fees, but they do earn the gratitude of
the professionals they select, and this gratitude has been
known to be negotiable in cash or its equivalent.

Electioneering begins anew at the committee meeting
with those strongly committed members doing their best
to influence the fence-sitters. This is done with more
speechmaking, as committee members extoll the qualifica-
tions and integrity of this attorney or that accountant.
There is also the quiet one-on-one negotiation—you vote
for my attorney and I'll vote for your accountant, or you
vote for my man this time and I'll vote for yours next
time.

The actual voting is on a free-form basis. Sometimes it's
done by closed ballot, sometimes by a show of hands;
sometimes the biggest creditor just says I want so-and-so
and that's it; sometimes three names are placed in nomi-
nation and if two get two votes each and the third gets
three votes, he's in. Sometimes an aggressive committee
member can force another ballot and, with the right

pressure in the right places, combine forces of the two-vote firms and take the case four to three.

The makeup of the committee, the degree of commitment, the ingenuity, aggressiveness and experience of the members will determine the procedure.

On the surface the action at a creditors' meeting appears spontaneous, but there is much advance preparation. When a meeting of creditors is about to be held, the news travels with incredible speed. The unofficial grapevine is a marvel of modern communication, and within minutes after a decision is made to call a creditors' meeting, the lawyers and accountants are on the telephone lining up votes. The meeting notice itself usually goes out about two or three days before the meeting date, so there's plenty of time for maneuvering.

Creditors' lists are circulated through unofficial channels, and the lawyers and accountants are soon poring over the lists, looking for familiar names. If the lawyers find the names of their own clients on the list, that's great. But just to make sure the client shows up, they'll get on the phone and remind him to appear. Every client that comes is a potential committee member and a potential vote.

If they find names of creditors they have met before or have had some dealings with in other cases, it's still worth a call to try to get support.

The conversation of necessity is a guarded one. It's unethical for an attorney to solicit a claim. The call would sound someting like this:

"Hello, Jack. This is Barney. You remember—Barney Greenglass. We were in the Plotnik bust together."

"Who?"

"You know, the Plotnik case. He tried to screw us with a lousy fifteen percent offer, but we worked him up to twenty-five."

"Oh, yeah. I remember now. You were for the creditors. That was a real stinkeroo."

"Right, Jack. But listen. There's a meeting coming up next week on Grobner's Stores and I see you're on the list. I've got a couple of claims in the case and have to go anyhow, so if you want me to cover for you, I'll be happy to do it. It won't cost you a cent."

"I'd be glad to let you represent me, Barney, but you're the fifth lawyer that's called me this morning. I already gave my claim to Arthur Flagler."

"That's O.K., Jack. Arthur's a great guy. One of the best in the business. Take care, Jack. Maybe I'll see you at the meeting."

So Barney hangs up and mumbles to himself what an unethical sonofabitch Flagler is and goes on to call the next name on the list.

On the next call, Barney could be luckier and get the claim or at least the word that the creditor would support him for committee counsel if the creditor's own lawyer doesn't stand a chance.

A creditors' meeting, as one veteran bankruptcy attorney puts it, draws lawyers like fruit flies around a rotten banana. The accountants don't normally show up at creditors' meetings since there's no function for them to perform there. Sometimes they come to shake a few hands, but generally they make their phone calls and sit back in the office, waiting to be summoned. In a typical case the accountant will know within minutes after a committee meeting is over who got the case and exactly what committee member voted for what accountant.

Attorneys, in addition to appearing on their own behalf, come to represent clients and, since they are trained in the art of public speaking and parliamentary procedure, tend to dominate most meetings.

Before the meeting gets under way, the attorneys gather in the meeting room and start lying to each other:

"I've got the six largest creditors, so what the hell are you even bothering with this for?"

This means he's got one small creditor and sees five familiar faces in the crowd.

Or, "I've got a two-hundred-thousand-dollar creditor and the whole case is only two hundred and fifty thousand. It's mine."

This his colleagues at the bar take to mean there's a $200,000 creditor in the case and he's up for grabs.

Or, "I hear you have a couple of big creditors. Why don't you join us? We may not be able to take this case, but we have enough to knock you out of it. Be smart. Together we can't lose."

This could be serious and is worth checking out.

When the lawyers aren't busy making deals with each other, they're running around the room shaking hands with creditors, trying to find out who's committed to whom and who the free agents are.

The politicking is so intense that even the attorneys with the big claims in their pockets still have to play the game to avoid the possibility of getting pushed out of a case.

There is no room for complacency at a large creditors' meeting. Many a lawyer who sat confidently by because he thought he had a case all wrapped up has been forced either to split his fee with the hustlers or finish completely out of the money.

"I remember a case," recalls an old-timer, "where Charlie Frederickson came in with a creditor who was far and away the top man. His client became chairman of an eleven-member committee.

"When the committee convened to pick a lawyer, the chairman said with the tone of a man who thought he was entitled, 'I'd like Frederickson to be our counsel.' The rest of the committee members just laughed, and when Frederickson refused to make a deal and take in a few partners, the committee voted him out and he wound up in the street. Didn't make a dime on the case.

"There was another time when I came into a meeting with six out of the ten largest creditors in the case. So I walk in and here's Al Catlet standing with a big cigar and a smile on his face and he says to me, 'What are you doing here? We got it all locked up.'

" 'Locked up?' I say. 'I have six out of the top ten.'

" 'You're kidding. We have the biggest creditor in the case and we got a bunch of little guys too. You better come in with us or you'll wind up sucking hind tit.'

" 'Don't give me that crap,' I said. 'This is my case.' And would you believe it, the sonsofbitches packed the committee and then offered me fifty percent of the deal. I told them to go screw and threatened to take my creditors and form my own committee. But when it was all over, I had to settle for sixty percent and cut them in for forty."

If there are two compatible attorneys who can control a case between them, they can go in as co-counsel to the creditors' committee. This is a completely legitimate arrangement. On occasion a nonaligned committee member may balk at having to pay for two lawyers, but this is not a serious problem. Someone will get up and explain that the committee is really getting two great legal minds for the price of one, so how can anyone complain? This will usually comfort the committeeman, unless he's just trying to make trouble so he can sneak his own man in.

The fact that the political balance of power can result in co-counselships suggests that perhaps in some cases the realities of power could result in three, four, five or more attorneys with a piece of the fees.

Since the bar association frowns on under-the-table fee-splitting among attorneys or attorneys and laymen, nobody will talk for the record about the practice. But take my word for it, there are lots of partnerships that never show up on the record.

Attorneys who operate this way are known in the trade as piecers. Since they haven't the power base to control cases, they'll hustle their way into a piece of it.

They'll come to a meeting with a small claim and try to pick up some more, or they'll sometimes come with no claims at all and hope to make enough noise and fuss to grab a part of the fee.

Once a group gets its man elected, a fee-splitting arrangement must be worked out. The formula is to give the attorney of record anywhere from 25 percent to one third off the top to cover the taxes on the full fee. The remainder is whacked up into as many slices as necessary. The man who delivered the most votes gets the biggest piece of the fee.

If I have given the impression so far that the reason for being on a creditors' committee is to provide fees for attorneys and accountants, that is not entirely erroneous.

However, the committee does have other functions. It must keep an eye on the debtor's operations to see that the remaining assets are not unduly dissipated, and it must look into the firm's financial condition, negotiate a settlement and then make its recommendations to the rest of the creditors.

This part of committee work is not nearly as much fun as picking lawyers and accountants. Everybody fights to get on a committee, but when it comes time to get down to work, a seventeen-member committee can easily dwindle to nine or ten.

The normal procedure is for the committee to have an audit done by its accountant so it has a point of reference for the negotiations. The accountant will come up with the liquidating value of the assets and the going concern value, the degree of honesty or dishonesty with which the debtor has conducted his business. It doesn't hurt the creditors' bargaining position if the accountant can show a couple of minor irregularities—a small loan paid off to a relative, overenthusiastic payments on obligations that were personally guaranteed by the owner of the debtor company. That sort of information provides leverage for the committee in working out a deal.

After hearing the accountant's report, the committee invites the debtor and his attorney down to a meeting and the bargaining begins. The debtor's attorney, who is ready to pay 40 percent, offers 35 percent. The committee, which wants 45 percent, asks for 50.

There's a lot of play-acting and hand-wringing and head-shaking as the debtor's attorney insists that 35 percent is the absolute top dollar and hints that his client will have to borrow from a vicious mother-in-law and an unconscionable loan shark to scrape together money for a 35 percent settlement.

The creditors, for their part, say that 50 cents is extremely generous, and if the debtor won't pay, they'll liquidate the business and sue him for the money he paid back to his sister just two weeks ago.

After these discussions are carried on for a respectable period, the debtor and his attorney will step out of the room for some private discussion, and in a few minutes they'll come back with a new offer.

"We've gone over these figures again and rechecked our possible money sources and here is my final offer—thirty-seven-and-a-half percent."

This will be greeted with utter disbelief by the creditors, who now will be ready to take 45 percent. But 37½—never.

Bargaining continues and finally a deal is reached—42½ percent. This is precisely halfway between the first offer and the committee's demand, and it might have been simpler just to split the difference when the figures were first mentioned, but negotiations must be carried on by traditional methods much like Oriental fertility rites.

Carl Schaeffer, who has been representing debtors in insolvency cases for forty years in New York's textile and apparel field, is the acknowledged master of the out-of-court settlement.

Schaeffer says he tries to give creditors a better deal than they would get in liquidation and, at the same time, see that "there's a little left" for the client. Over the years about 90 percent of the insolvency cases he's taken on were settled successfully, and the overwhelming majority were concluded without resorting to court proceedings.

He thinks that too many bankruptcy lawyers take the wrong approach in dealing with creditors.

"The average lawyer thinks the cheapest deal is best for his client. That doesn't work with a sophisticated creditor body. A lawyer who comes in with a first offer of fifteen percent and then gets dragged up to sixty-five percent loses all around. His client thinks he's incompetent, the creditors make him pay through the nose and they don't have any respect for the lawyer or the client. Everybody loses. To start with, fifteen cents in a case like that is nonsense.

"I figure out the liquidation value and how long it will take for creditors to get their money. How much and how long. There's a big difference between a buck today and having to wait a year for it, and the creditors know it. Then I figure out what the business is worth to the client and split the difference. That way, everyone gets more. If the deal calls for sixty-five cents, I start five or ten percent less so that for psychological reasons the creditors can think they are getting me to improve my offer.

"Also, I play square and follow the rules. I don't grab a fee and shoot out notices of meetings. There were lots of times that I didn't even take a fee at the outset and relied on the creditors' committee to give me my fee."

Getting back to the function of the committee, in out-of-court cases, it has the final say on fees for the attorneys, the accountants and the secretary. This is another reason the committee members get the VIP treatment from the professionals.

Once an agreement is reached, the committee counsel works up a formal contract, embodying the settlement terms, and when this is signed a letter goes out to all creditors. The letter points out that the committee has looked into the debtor's business affairs and has come up with the best possible settlement for creditors. The letter goes on to urge all creditors to file written acceptances of the offer.

In an out-of-court settlement, substantially all creditors must accept if the deal is to go through. The theory is that everyone must be treated equally. Either everyone takes the 55 percent or whatever, or the case goes into the bankruptcy courts, where there are legal standards designed for the equitable distribution of assets.

In the real world, though, there are always those who want to be treated more equally than others.

Small creditors who don't have much to lose if a settlement falls through will often insist on getting paid in full, and they stand a pretty good chance of getting it, too. In a deal involving a million dollars or so, it doesn't make sense to let a few thousand dollars in small claims tear it apart.

There's also the chiseler who wants an extra 10 percent on the side to get his vote and threatens to sue for his entire claim and kill the settlement if he doesn't get his way. These, according to attorneys who try to hold settlements together, are handled on a case-by-case basis. Factors to be considered are the size of the claim and whether there is any justification for the special treatment. Then they decide whether it's more practical to pay or fight.

The insolvency field comprises a pretty tight-knit group, and anyone who makes a habit of screwing up settlements with demands for special treatment will find other creditors waiting for an opportunity to shove it to him. If, for instance, the habitual chiseler gets caught very big in an insolvency and a busted-up settlement would be extremely costly to him, that's when the other creditors decide that they don't want to do business and go ahead with their lawsuits.

There are defenses against a creditor who won't go along with a settlement that the rest of the creditors want. One is Chapter XI. If a settlement is stalled because of a couple of recalcitrant creditors, the debtor can file under Chapter XI and consummate a settlement if he gets a simple majority to accept. If the required majority says yes, the rest of the creditors must take the proposal whether they like it or not.

(The required majority covers both the number of creditors and the amount of their claims. Thus if there are 100 claims filed for a total of $1 million, at least fifty-one creditors with a total indebtedness of over $500,000 must accept. Also, there are technical objections nonconsenting creditors can bring to oppose a plan, but if the plan is fair and there has been no fraud, the majority rules.)

Once a settlement is completed, either out of court or in Chapter XI, there is no longer any legal obligation on the debtor's part to pay the balance of his old debt. The settlement is in full payment of the original obligation.

It's unfair to try to get your old debt paid in full when everyone else has taken a licking, but if you have the leverage, why not?

Suppose you have a particularly hot line of merchandise that your old debtor must have if he ever hopes to make a go of his newly refinanced business. So you tell him, "You want my stuff, pay up what you stuck me for in your last bust. I'll even arrange easy terms. Instead of paying me ten dollars a dozen for it, which is the regular price, I'll bill you at twelve dollars a dozen and the extra two bucks will go toward paying off the old debt. When that's repaid, then I'll go back to charging ten dollars."

The beauty of this kind of arrangement is that nobody except you and the customer knows that the old debt is being paid back. The records merely show a simple buyer-seller relationship.

Leverage is the key. If the seller has enough, he can force the buyer to bend. If it's a buyer's market, the seller will have to shrug off his loss and hope to make it back through future dealings.

4 You Have to Give a Bankrupt Credit

There are two sides to every bankruptcy. On one side is the company that buys more than it can pay for, and on the other are the credit men for the suppliers who let it happen.

The credit man plays a pivotal position in the game. His job is to see that his company gets paid for whatever it sells. But if he never gets stuck, his boss thinks the credit man is being too conservative, approving only the sure things and thus probably passing up a lot of business that a more liberal credit policy would generate.

If the credit man gets caught too often, then he's criticized for gross stupidity. "How could you ship this guy? Any idiot could see he was going busted," says the boss, who is possessed of extraordinary vision after the creditors'-meeting notice arrives.

It is also the credit man's job to try to salvage what he can from a sour credit. In some of the more stable fields of business, in which three or four giants dominate, credit losses are no great problem. If your principal customers are General Motors and United States Steel, you don't have too many bad debts. But if you sell to hundreds of small dress manufacturers or thousands of retailers around the country, credit and its proper administration becomes significant.

The importance of credit granting, particularly in the volatile textile-apparel business, has been at the heart of the growth of factoring, and factors are very much in the middle of the insolvency business.

Factors are probably the most misunderstood of America's business organizations. The popular impression of a factor is a company that lends money at outrageous rates and forecloses mortgages a lot. This unflattering image developed, in part, because there are many small firms operating on the fringes of legitimacy that call themselves factors, charge outrageous rates and foreclose mortgages a lot.

A lawyer makes a few bucks and he'd like to turn a little, so he puts a sign on his office door—FINK FACTORS—and he starts lending money at 25 percent per annum.

There are also many commercial finance companies that make secured loans and call themselves factors. These are perfectly legitimate enterprises that charge higher interest rates than banks do because the loans they make are riskier and more expensive to administer. But they are not factors as the word is defined by the purists in the industry.

The factor (referred to in the trade as "old line" factor to distinguish it from a commercial finance company) is essentially a service organization that sells credit guarantees for a fee. The mechanics involve the purchase of their clients' accounts receivable. They also lend money, as advances against receivables they buy and as unsecured over-advances. And they charge higher rates than banks do because they are really wholesalers of money. They borrow money from the banks at the prevailing bank rate and then relend it at a markup in the same way that any other commodity is bought and resold at a profit. In recent years the banks themselves have taken over most of the old-line factors, but the factoring divisions of the banks continue to operate in the traditional manner.

It's the credit guarantee that gets the factors into so many insolvencies. In 1971 the factoring industry guaranteed some $13 billion in credit extended by clients. Bad debt losses of about two tenths of 1 percent are regarded as reasonable, so we're dealing with $26 million worth of bad debts.

Incidentally, if you're a factor, it's no catastrophe to get caught on some bad credits as long as the bad debts don't get out of hand. In fact, it's imperative to get hung up once in a while if a factor wants to be able to sell its services.

Their major pitch to prospective clients is "Why go through all the expense of running a credit department and take the risk of losing money on bad debts when you can let us do all your credit checking for you? And if we approve the credit, we'll guarantee that you'll get paid even if your customer doesn't pay us." The fee for this service runs anywhere from a fraction of 1 percent of sales to over 2 percent, depending on the size of the client's invoices, his overall volume and the nature of the receivables.

Prospective clients are a suspicious lot and argue that a factor could adopt a policy of approving only sales to Sears, Roebuck or J. C. Penney and turn the riskier customers down. The factor, therefore, must be able to show that he is willing to stick his neck out for a client and take a reasonable share of credit losses.

Because of the nature of their business, the factors get stuck frequently, and their credit men are hip-deep in the insolvencies field.

Some factors have specialists whose principal job is to follow up on bad debts. They go to creditors' meetings, get elected to creditors' committees, vote for the selection of attorneys and accountants, negotiate for settlements and pass on the fees of the committee's professional staff.

Some factors let the credit man responsible for approving the bum credit follow through himself. In addition to the factors, the large textile mills have substantial bad-debt problems. Their credit men are frequent visitors at 71 West 23rd Street, the offices of the New York Credit Men's Adjustment Bureau, where most textile-apparel creditors' meetings are held.

There are also a couple of credit insurance companies whose representatives show up regularly at creditors' meetings. American Credit Indemnity Company and London Guarantee & Accident Company insure accounts receivable and handle the follow-up work on bad credits for their clients.

The insurance representatives, just like the adjustment specialists at the factors, have nothing to do with the original extension of the credit, and they take a professional approach to the problem at hand.

A credit man whose losses run too high will soon find himself out of a job, but the specialists can go to creditors' meetings every day—many of them do—and still not be concerned about job security. It is these professionals and those credit men who are expected to have a reasonable volume of bad debts that are most admired and romanced by the lawyers and accountants looking for insolvency work.

Credit men dealing day to day with thousands of customers are good business sources for lawyers and accountants.

A credit man trying to collect a past-due bill may discover that his customer is really in trouble and needs a bankruptcy lawyer.

"Why don't you go see my friend Joe Clopchick? He knows his business and will be able to get you straightened out." Joe Clopchick, the lawyer, will be most grateful for that kind of recommendation.

Or take the customer who wants a large line of credit. The credit man is nervous about it, so he says, "If you really want a fifty-thousand-dollar line, you'll have to get a new accountant. I don't know your accountant from left field and I'd be more comfortable if you put Jerry Blatz on the books." Jerry Blatz will also be more comfortable and will think nice thoughts about the credit man who recommended him.

Credit men who go to meetings are not always free agents. They often go with instructions from their firms. "I have to vote for my firm's attorney, but I have my choice of accountants," says one of the specialists.

Others are free to vote as they please.

How do they decide who will be their choice? They vote for the professionals they think will do the best job and for the ones that they owe favors to and for the ones they feel will be most grateful.

"Competence is way down on the bottom of my list

when it comes to deciding on what accountant or lawyer I should vote for," says one veteran of the creditors'-meeting crowd, only half joking. "I think friendship is probably at the top."

Friendship is a highly complex concept. Some credit men are friendly to accountants or lawyers because they like their personalities or because of past favors.

Most of the graft that goes on in the business is of the honest kind—lunches, dinners, theater tickets, parties, convention trips, golf outings and Christmas gifts. These have become generally acceptable practices in business relationships.

A credit man I know swears that a colleague was once presented with a $45,000 house by a grateful accountant. The lucky credit man had been responsible for sending over a client that netted the accountant a $250,000 fee.

There are also reports of cash payoffs. A lawyer who was once with a credit insurance company says that he was offered bribes time and again to vote for cheap settlements.

"I never took any," he said, "but I know of some fellow who got two truckloads of furniture for voting in favor of a twenty-five percent settlement in a case that called for thirty-five percent.

"It's really very tempting for a credit man or insurance-company employee who is working for peanuts and representing claims that run into six figures to bend his principles a little, vote for a cheap settlement and get more for his one vote than he earns in a year. Supervisors must be careful as hell to review settlements and make sure the company is getting a fair shake from the credit man representing it at the meeting."

The recurring theme is that "I don't take payoffs," "I

don't give payoffs, but the other guy is on the take," or "my competitor gets his business by paying off."

An adjustment specialist for one of the major factoring firms told me, "I've been in this business a lot of years and I've never been offered a payoff. I hear these stories, but it never happened to me. Sure, they take me to lunch and they invite me to parties, but I've never been offered any money. I also heard stories about collection agencies— that they pay credit men to steer collection business their way. Do you know how much money there is in the collection business? They get twenty-five percent of the first two thousand dollars and twenty percent of the balance. With some factors doing a volume in billions, there's a lot of money there."

Which brings me to the role of the collection man in the insolvency business. When a credit man feels a collection is getting sticky and he thinks he needs help with it, he'll turn the claim over to a collection agency. The agent will have a go at collecting, and if he can't get results, he forwards the claim to an attorney who will bring suit, if necessary.

Collection costs vary, depending on how far the claim is carried before collection. Over the years, credit men estimate that they net about 50 cents on the dollar.

"By the time all the fees and court costs and the like are taken care of, we're lucky to get half a buck," says one credit man.

This, by the way, is considerably better than the overall return on claims in insolvency proceedings. Lumping together bankruptcies, Chapter XIs, assignments, out-of-court settlements—the whole gamut—the return is between 20 and 25 percent.

When a collection agent gets a number of claims

against the same debtor, he knows that there is something drastically wrong with the debtor's business, and the collection man is in a position to get the ball rolling for an insolvency proceeding. The agent might just suggest one of his favorite bankruptcy attorneys to handle the case or he could put the whole package together himself.

In fact, if he's real good, he can even tell the debtor beforehand what kind of a settlement he can get through.

But again, ask any collection agent in town, and he says he's heard about all these setups but he wouldn't think of doing such a thing. "All I do is what my clients—the creditors—ask me to do" is the stock reply.

They will concede that the conditions exist for taking advantage of a situation.

"If I get a bunch of claims against a company and see that the money just isn't there," says an old-time master of the art of shaking loose the elusive buck, "I tell him he'd better see his lawyer and think about calling the creditors together. At this point I'm in a position to control the deal. The debtor is harassed and bewildered and I look like the only friend he's got. But that's not the way I work. I've never been to a creditors' meeting in my life.

"But there are collection agents who handle the meeting of creditors and get a fee as committee secretary, bring in attorneys for the debtor and for the creditors, work a deal with an auctioneer and collect fees from everybody. There are some who will even guarantee a cheap settlement, and with their influence over the creditors and the creditors' attorneys, they can pull it off. In these cases, let's say an estate owes two hundred thousand dollars and should pay fifty percent. Instead, a twenty-five percent settlement is pushed through, so there's a profit

of fifty thousand dollars to be sliced up. The usual procedure is for the collection agent and the lawyer for the
creditors to split up half the profit and for the debtor to
keep the other half. Everybody makes money except the
creditors."

Another link that leads from early financial problems to
the bankruptcy courts or the out-of-court adjustment is
the sales promoter.

There are a number of them operating in various parts
of the country, and their business is to run highly promotional sales for retailers on a commission basis. For a
percentage of the gross, they undertake to hype up a
floundering retailer's business. Since many of the retailers
serviced by sales promoters are on the brink of bankruptcy, the promoters often function as liquidators.

They run these "MUST RAISE CASH IN A HURRY" sales, or
"GOING OUT OF BUSINESS" sales that seem interminable.

When these promoters get involved with a merchant
who appears insolvent, they know the ropes well enough
to set up a creditors' meeting, work out a settlement and
then run a sale—either to raise money or to pay off a settlement and keep the business going or just to liquidate out
and take their cut.

After a firm has gone through with an out-of-court
settlement or a Chapter XI proceeding, its subsequent
survival depends on the ability to get credit. Some suppliers have blanket prohibitions against extending new
credit to any company that has gone through an insolvency proceeding.

There wouldn't be much point to settlements with
creditors if there was no possibility of getting credit, and
a good bankruptcy lawyer can help.

Here's one leading practitioner's method:

"I ask my client what credit man he was most friendly with before the recent unpleasantness. I tell the client to go see the credit man, explain that the business has been refinanced and ask for just a little credit—maybe five hundred bucks. If the credit man agrees and the client gets the five hundred, I advise my man to anticipate. Whatever the terms of sale are, pay early. Then, still working with the same credit man, I tell the client to ask for a thousand or maybe fifteen hundred and repay that early too.

"Next, I suggest that another former supplier be approached and told 'Charlie's giving me a fifteen-hundred line of credit. What about you?' Soon there are enough suppliers giving him credit that he can go anywhere. In any business, it's very tough for a credit man to justify turning an account down if all his competitors are checking it."

A credit man can also rationalize the extension of new credit on the basis of post-settlement figures. Once a settlement has been effected and old debts scaled down or wiped out, the emerging business looks great on paper—virtually no debt and all the assets intact. When a credit man's boss asks how the hell he can check anyone who has just gone broke, the answer is "Now he's good."

5 Bankruptcies Add Up for Accountants

The bankruptcy accountant is a special breed. He constantly complains that he loses money on bankruptcy work, but he'll cajole, harangue, plead, beg, threaten and sometimes, yes, even step into the twilight zone between business promotion and bribery to land a sizable insolvency case.

There are several reasons accountants are so anxious to get these cases. For one thing, accountants, just like attorneys, have these stuffy ethical codes about not advertising. So if they become accountants for creditors in large bankruptcies, they stand a good chance of having their names bandied about in the trade papers and sometimes even in the consumer press. Thus they not only get advertising, but it's free and doesn't violate the letter of the no-advertising strictures.

Also, bankruptcy work is a good source of new business. An accounting firm going in to do an audit of a financially troubled company may get to keep the company as a client if it is rehabilitated.

And finally, they don't lose money on bankruptcy work.

They may occasionally take a loss on a no-asset case, but the credit man who sticks them with the bomb will make it up the next time. That is, he'd better if he ever wants to be invited to the accountant's golf club again. Bankruptcy accountants, incidentally, are among the best golfers in the business world because they have to spend so much time on the course entertaining credit men.

It's not all fun and games, though. Accountants in the insolvencies area must develop special skills for investigative audits. As you have probably gathered by now, the business methods used by the more inventive bankrupts are not covered by the generally accepted accounting principles of the American Institute of Certified Public Accountants. The accountant dealing in adjustments must know what to look for and be able to guide creditors in their negotiations.

They must be able to spot entries that are somehow not in keeping with the normal operation of a business.

For instance, an accountant with lots of years in the business tells of one case in which he picked up an inordinate number of payments for interior decorating. The company had a modest showroom, and the amount of money being spent for interior decorating would have paid for a lobby at the Lincoln Center for the Performing Arts.

The accountant confronted the owner of the business with the canceled checks and asked what all this interior decorating was about.

"They're payments for decorating my showroom," the executive explained.

"Come now," said the accountant. "That crummy showroom of yours couldn't possibly cost this much money and, besides, you make these payments pretty regularly. You don't expect me to believe you redecorate your showroom every couple of months. You'd better come clean with me or I'll make it rough for you with the creditors. What have you been doing, decorating your home and charging it to the company?"

The businessman flushed a little and then confessed, "No, I haven't been using the money for myself, but I'll tell you where the payments go. You see, in my business I have to entertain buyers and I have to fix some of them up with girls. So I found one of the town's most reliable madams, had her register down at the county clerk's office as an interior decorator, and when I send my customers up to her place she bills me for interior-decorating service."

Since accounting in the insolvencies field is so specialized, it's only natural that most of this work would be concentrated within a small group of accounting firms. Most of the large national firms are not set up for bankruptcy work and, at least as far as the specialists say, wouldn't know how to handle it anyhow.

There are, however, two major firms—S. D. Leidesdorf & Company and J. K. Lasser & Company—that are active in insolvencies. Leidesdorf's entry into the business is due largely to one man—Gerald D. Stone, who spent ten years (1931–41) as a staff man at the New York Credit Men's Adjustment Bureau and who joined Leidesdorf after World War II. The contacts he had made while working at the Bureau provided him with a nucleus for steering adjustment work to Leidesdorf.

Mr. Stone, a super charm merchant who looks like an Ivy League cherub constantly fighting and losing a battle against overweight, has since expanded his contacts to reach up to the top echelon of just about every major bank in New York City. Banks are prime sources of insolvency and other accounting business.

Mr. Stone has also climbed ahead at Leidesdorf and is now managing partner of an organization with 100 partners and a staff of over 1,000.

At this stage, Leidesdorf picks and chooses the adjustment cases it will handle and rarely will take anything that doesn't fall into the seven-figure category.

Lasser broke into the field in the late 1960s through the absorption of a small accounting firm called Farmer, Maimone & Braun. The partners in the smaller firm—Jerome Farmer, Dominick Maimone and Melvin Braun—were active in the textile-apparel credit community and when they became partners in Lasser were able to attract insolvency business there.

Clarence Rainess & Company, a fairly large accounting firm which has a clientele concentrated in the soft-goods fields (Jonathan Logan and Bobbie Brooks are among the Rainess firm's publicly owned apparel clients), is another of the accounting firms with expertise in the bankruptcy business.

Others include Hertz, Herson & Company; Kipnis, Karchmer, Meyerson & Levine; Joseph S. Herbert & Company; Laventhol, Krekstein, Horwath & Horwath; Simonoff, Peyser & Citrin; Aronson & Oresman and Herbert H. Levess & Company; Fred Landau & Company; Roberts & Leinwander Company; A. Jesse Goldstein & Company; and Leon I. Radin & Company.

The basic function of the accountant retained by creditors is to get an independent appraisal of the financial condition of the debtor and to check on whether or not the business was conducted with reasonable honesty. Creditors being asked to forgive a portion of their claims want to find out what happened to their money and also want some assurance that the figures they are working with in determining a settlement are for real.

In out-of-court settlements, there's no problem hiring accountants or paying their fees because the creditors' committee will see that the auditors get paid. In fact, if a case is about to blow up and wind up in the bankruptcy courts, the committee will do its utmost to get the accountant his fee before any court papers are filed.

"We try to see that the accountants get paid," says one credit man, "because their outlay is largely labor. They have to send men down to do the work. If a case goes into bankruptcy, the lawyers can always get their fees out as attorney for the trustee or something like that, but the accountants don't get anything if the court doesn't appoint them."

Another point that bugs the accountants in the insolvencies business is the precedence of the bar. Ask any accountant and he'll tell you that the whole court system is stacked in favor of the lawyers. The judges and referees are all lawyers and naturally feel a kinship for their fellow barristers. For their part, some lawyers think accountants are just a bunch of college-educated bookkeepers who perform a purely mechanical function. There was one referee I remember who was particularly down on accountants, and whenever there was a request for an accountant he'd turn it down out of hand and suggest that the records be brought to the courtroom and he'd tell them anything they wanted to know. Several accountants mumbled threats of someday backing up a moving van full of records and dumping them in the court, but to my knowledge none ever made good on the threat.

On the other hand, there are lawyers who like to see accountants get good fees, at least in out-of-court settlements. There's a kind of unwritten code setting forth the relationship between the fee for the attorney and that of the CPA—something in the neighborhood of 3 to 2 (the lawyer gets the 3). So if the CPA asks for $500, the attorney isn't going to be able to get away with $5,000. In that type of situation, the attorney might just encourage the accountant to think more highly of the professional standing of the certified public accountant.

"Shmuck," he'll say, "how the hell am I supposed to make a decent pay day in this case when you're asking for a chintzy five hundred dollars? Smarten up and next time ask for three grand. The committee'll knock you down to twenty-five hundred and you'll still be better off and I'll be able to make a few bucks too."

Whether it's a bankruptcy case or out-of-court settlement, the function of the accountant is fundamentally the same: He must find out where and what all the assets are and verify the liabilities. He also looks for irregularities to determine if there are any grounds for criminal prosecution or for suits to recover funds for the benefit of creditors.

In spite of the almost boundless talents of financially distressed businessmen for covering up under-the-table activities, the experienced bankruptcy accountant has seen most of them before. High on the list of shady bankruptcy practices are preferential payments. These are payments that would give one creditor a better shake than others in the same class. Experience has shown that the first place to look for preferential payments is in the account of the owner. The second would be his relatives' accounts.

Repaid bank loans are also carefully examined. Bank loans to small and medium-sized companies are usually personally guaranteed by the principals of the business, so it's smart to pay the bank off while holding back payments to creditors who do not hold guarantees.

A favorite practice of banks is to offset deposits against unpaid loan balances whenever they get the feeling that the customer may be in trouble. (When a bank makes a loan, the borrower is normally required to maintain an account with the lending bank.) Once a bank exercises its right of offset, checks start bouncing all over the neighborhood and the customer is forced to go to his creditors or the bankruptcy courts for help.

While it's perfectly legal for a bank to grab any money in a customer's account and credit it against an unpaid loan, this right is subject to abuse.

A company in financial trouble can, with the connivance of his banker, build up deposits by not paying his other creditors, and one fine day the bank offsets.

After the bank cleans out the account, the debtor can run to his other creditors and tell them how he had every intention of paying them all in full but this rotten bank took all his cash. Meanwhile, he's off the hook on the personal guarantee, the bank has its money back and other creditors are left with an empty feeling in their lower intestines.

Creditors expect their accountant to spot such goings on and give their attorney enough information to hang a lawsuit on. In order to get anywhere in a suit to get a bank to put back a preferential payment, there must be proof that the bank knew or had reasonable cause to believe its customer was insolvent and that there was collusion between the customer and the bank to give the bank preferred treatment.

Preferential payments are not easy to prove, so the rule of thumb among credit men and bankers is that such payments are inexcusable if the other fellow gets one, but if you can get a preference, take the money and run.

Preferences can also come in the form of extra collateral or the return of merchandise.

A key element in any action for return of a preferential payment is proof that the debtor was insolvent at the time of the payment and the beneficiary knew or had reasonable cause to believe the debtor was insolvent.

Elliot Meisel of Roberts & Leinwander Company, who has had lots of experience searching for preferential payments, illustrates this with a rather macabre incident:

A commercial stationery company ran into problems and decided to create its own invoices without worrying too much about whether or not there were any sales to back them up. The invoices were turned over to a finance company for cash advances. When the finance company discovered the invoices were of questionable authenticity, it persuaded the client to turn over a $100,000 insurance policy on the life of one of the officers. The officer promptly stepped in front of a train and was killed.

A bankruptcy followed, and the trustee showed that the finance company had audited the client's books every month and had run off a statement showing the client was insolvent just before the transfer of the insurance policy. The court ordered the insurance money turned over to the bankruptcy estate.

The accountant must also search for missing assets. Automobiles have a habit of disappearing with remarkable regularity. A company car seems to be standard equipment for every business, no matter how small the operation. The car will be paid for by the company, insured by the company and enjoyed by the company principals. But when the bankruptcy comes, the car somehow turns out to be registered in the name of one of the officers as his personal property. By checking payment records, the accountant can establish that the car is in fact the property of the business.

Efforts by officers of bankrupt companies to sneak off with the company car are really in the nature of petty larceny. The big action is in inventory. This can run into real money.

The system for tracing missing inventory is fairly simple in concept. The accountant checks sales against purchases and comes up with a figure of what should be left over. For instance, a new business that starts out with zero inventory, buys $100,000 worth and sells $50,000 should have $50,000 worth of goods left.

That's the concept, but in practice there are all kinds of complicating factors. There's markup to be figured and off-price sales, and one of the biggest problems is getting a starting point.

In most cases, the business has been around too long for the auditor to trace back to the inception of the company, and he must start with an inventory as reported in a financial statement issued by the debtor.

Missing inventory can be explained in several ways.

The simplest is that the goods were either just diverted by the principals of the business or stolen by third parties unknown; or inventory has been sold for cash and sales not recorded; or inventory was sold below cost; or the inventory shown in the financial statement used as a starting point just wasn't there.

If, for example, inventory was shown at $100,000 on the statement, purchases since the statement date were $50,000 and sales $100,000, there should be $50,000 worth of goods left. (For simplicity we're ignoring markup.) If there were only $10,000 left, there are two possible explanations—either $40,000 worth of inventory disappeared between the statement date and the bankruptcy or the financial statement inflated the inventory in the first place. In either case, creditors would want to look further into the matter.

Below-cost selling in legitimate arm's-length transactions may be bad business, but there's nothing illegal about it. But selling below cost can be used illegally to divert inventory of a company about to go broke.

A failing corporation can sell its merchandise at absurdly low prices to a new corporation set up by the owners of the outfit about to bust. Merchandise might also be sold below cost to relatives or close friends.

The accountant must look into suspicious-looking sales by checking prices on sales made close to the bankruptcy with prices charged, say, six months earlier. He also looks into the buyers who are the beneficiaries of these cut-rate sales.

T & E (travel and entertainment) is another handy instrument for pulling assets out of a business before turning over the remains to the creditors. Mr. Meisel says that he has found such unbusiness expenses as European vacations, personal clothing, family hotel and restaurant bills and similar items all charged to the company as business expenses. While this may sound like penny-ante stuff, he cites a case in which $125,000 a year was drained out of a business through the T & E route.

Works of art also have been known to vanish since they are easily moved and not exactly standard equipment for the average business. Mr. Meisel tells of a bankrupt who had some valuable paintings in his office, but when the auctioneer arrived to set up the bankruptcy sale they were gone.

Nobody would have been the wiser, but this man had been so eager to impress the world with his stature as a collector of fine art that everyone who had come into his showroom was sure to get the grand tour of the corporate art gallery. Consequently, the paintings were missed, the corporate records showed that they had been purchased with company funds and the lover of French Impressionism was forced to turn over his art treasures.

It is within the accountant's province, of course, to determine if a bankrupt has issued a false financial statement. A fraudulent statement can be the basis for blocking the discharge from bankruptcy of individuals or partnership and thus prevent them from getting out from under the debts. In the case of a corporation, the officer responsible for issuing a false statement (and sometimes his accountant) can be subject to criminal prosecution. If the statement has been transmitted through the mail, Federal mail-fraud statutes come into play.

A false financial statement is calculated to con suppliers into extending credit when the actual figures would bring a "no credit" rating.

It normally involves an overstatement of assets, an

understatement of liabilities or a combination of both. Sometimes the figures are pulled out of the air, but usually the practitioners of ultracreative accounting are more subtle.

For example, the statement might show receivables from affiliated companies or from other deadbeat companies that are really worthless. Or it may show an accurate evaluation of inventory but neglect to list unpaid bills covering part of that inventory. Or the bank balance listed in the statement might check out with the bank's records on the statement date, but a whole string of checks could be outstanding that had not yet cleared the bank. The bills covered by these checks of course would be treated as paid.

The accountant who knows his business can spot these little liberties and pass the information on to the creditors.

Drumming up new insolvency business is an important part of the accountant's work and a good deal of it comes from the credit men and from attorneys in the field. There is a form of reciprocity between the attorneys and the accountants. The lawyers are often in a position to recommend clients to the accountants and vice versa.

Aside from buying lunch and taking credit men out to the golf course, there are other ways in which accountants repay credit men for insolvency business. If an accountant has a client who could use factoring or financing service, he'll direct him to one of his more helpful credit men. Although credit men don't normally earn commissions on new business, they are always happy to score a few points by bringing in new accounts.

Accountants can also help credit men evaluate the credit risks of the CPA's own clients. Accountants have even gone so far as to guarantee personally the credit of a client, although this is the exception, not the rule.

For the record, credit men insist that they make their judgments independently, and no accountant tells them whose credit to approve and whose to turn down. But it's much easier to call a friendly accountant about one of his clients and just ask if it's O.K. to ship than it is to wade through page after page of dreary financial information in order to make a credit decision. The accountant knows his client's condition, and more than one credit man has made use of this convenient credit-checking technique. Again, for the record, the accountants maintain that all they do is give the credit man the facts and leave the decision-making up to him.

Even more off the record is the accountant who calls a particularly good friend in the credit field and says, "You never heard it from me, but one of my guys is in trouble. He's got inventory coming out of his ears and I suggest you get out as quickly as possible."

"Who is it?"

"I can't tell you who it is, but you're in it for thirty-five thousand."

This sort of phone call would drive the ethics committee of the New York Society of Certified Public Accountants up the wall, but ethics are sometimes trampled in the practicalities of business survival.

Suppose it had been the accountant who put the credit man into this overinventoried dog in the first place. The CPA would be in trouble and stand to lose a valuable contact. By tipping the credit man off, the accountant has further ingratiated himself and might expect favorable consideration the next time the tipee gets on a creditors' committee.

The pre-creditors'-meeting phone calls are used by accountants to remind credit men of their availability. Some accountants use the soft sell and just say something like "It would be nice if you put my name up," while others are more direct. "I want this case" is the way one accountant approaches potential committee members.

Conceding that he gets calls from accountants, a credit man I know says the most frequent approach is "I hear you're a creditor in Glop Company. Do me a favor and put my name in the hopper."

"I have no choice in picking an attorney. I have to vote for the firm that my company has on retainer. But I do have about five or six accounting firms that I select from. They all know their business and do a good job. If I picked accountant A at one meeting, I'll pick accountant B at the next and C after that.

"If a fellow calls me up and it's his turn, I might say, 'O.K., I was going to vote for you anyhow.' But if it's not his turn, then he's not getting my vote."

As for kickbacks, he says he never gets them and is perfectly happy with the lunches, golf outings and the occasional recommendations for his firm's new business department.

Others tell of $1,000 bar installations or $200 suits for credit men, paid for by grateful accountants.

But the typical accountant's comment goes like this:

"I know there are kickbacks in this business but I just don't give them. I take people out, I send out a few Christmas presents and I might do some personal income taxes for free, but I'm not going to get mixed up with payoffs."

Human nature being what it is, the urge to express gratitude in some concrete form will never be stamped out by professional societies and their codes of ethics. One of the most successful accountants in the business, in a moment of rare candor, explained it to me in the simplest, human terms: "If a credit man gets me a case that earns me a ten-thousand-dollar fee, what am I supposed to do? Just say thank you?"

6 Why Bankruptcy Lawyers Never Go Bankrupt

Attorneys in the bankruptcy field are looked upon by some of their colleagues at the bar as standing several rungs below the ambulance-chasing negligence lawyer. But this view does the bankruptcy practitioner a gross injustice. He is a specialist in a rough-and-tumble business, and, by and large, he'll perform as well as the attorneys in any other specialized field. He'll scratch for a fee with the best of them, and in his own specialty he will take on any general practitioner and send him back to his Wall Street office beaten and bloodied.

As a class, I think bankruptcy lawyers and other lawyers fall into five categories—honest, reasonably honest, reasonably dishonest, dishonest and very dishonest. (The alert reader might notice a lack of symmetry in these categories since there is a classification for very dishonest but none for very honest. This is not an oversight. No one who was very honest would ever choose to be a lawyer.)

New York, as the financial center of the country, is also the bankruptcy center and the attorneys know their business. They know the referees, they know each other, they know the clerks and they know the law. The first three areas of knowledge are perhaps more important than the last.

They know the referees' idiosyncrasies. One referee used to throw legal papers back at lawyers if Long Island was abbreviated instead of spelled out. "What's L.I. mean?" he'd growl. "I don't know what that means. What does N.Y. mean? Take these back and have them drawn up properly."

This same referee had a thing about differentiating between debtor-in-possession and debtor, a subtle distinction that can easily elude an attorney without much experience in the insolvency field. But the referee would run you out of his courtroom if you'd dare confuse the two.

Bankruptcy men also know the referees' attitudes. Some referees hate accountants and won't sign orders for their retention. Some are sympathetic toward bankrupts and antagonistic to creditors, while others lean in the other direction. Members of the club play each referee (in Manhattan there are four) with virtuoso skills.

Referee Asa S. Herzog is of the firm opinion that the bankruptcy bar requires knowledge that the general practitioner couldn't possibly have.

"Bankruptcy is a highly specialized field, and the best thing a general practitioner can do for his client is send him to a specialist."

He cites the case of a nonbankruptcy lawyer defending a young lady whose discharge from bankruptcy was being challenged by a small-loan company.

"The loan company showed that the girl had signed a false statement in applying for the loan. Her lawyer went after the loan-company clerk and tried to make him look like a worm. But I had to deny her discharge because the lawyer didn't make the right moves.

"Had he known his business, he would have pressed the question of reliance. Did the loan company actually rely on that statement in granting the loan or did they rely on her past record? She had borrowed from the company on five previous occasions and repaid those loans. She had a great record with them. I think if he'd worked on that point, he could have sold me.

"The attorney probably read the pertinent portion of the bankruptcy law, but, not knowing the case law, the importance of reliance just never occurred to him. Also, he kept his client off the stand, as though she were in a criminal case. I think if the case were properly presented, I might have granted her a discharge."

Then there is the question of getting quick action when needed on papers filed. A lawyer who knows the bankruptcy clerks will find he can get much better service than someone who walks in off the street. A busy bankruptcy clerk's office is no different from any other bureaucracy, and a stranger can spend a lot of valuable time being shoved from one clerk to another.

In addition to the individual leanings of the referees, the bankruptcy lawyers also know each other's peculiarities and know whom they can trust with what and whom they can rely on to say one thing and do another.

Bankruptcy lawyers are an earthy group and speak their own language.

As one practitioner puts it, "A couple of bankruptcy lawyers can get together, cuss each other out, and when they're finished they've got a deal that makes sense. But get one of those Wall Street firms and there'll be beautiful stationery and writs that could hang from the walls of Harvard Law School, but those creeps just don't know what the hell bankruptcy is about."

And while most nonbankruptcy lawyers don't know much about bankruptcy, they all know about forwarding fees, and this little device goes a long way toward keeping the bankruptcy practice in the province of the specialist. An attorney who forwards a case to a specialist is entitled to one third of the specialist's fee. Under the American Bar Association's rules of ethics, a forwarding attorney must actively participate in the case in order to qualify for a share of the fee.

As my mother would say, "They should live so long." The participation of forwarding attorneys in bankruptcy cases is often limited to phone calls by the forwarder, who wants to know how big the fee is going to be and when the hell the case is going to be closed out so he can collect his money.

There are situations in which the forwarding attorney can be of assistance to the specialist, and the forwarder with a conscience will go out of his way to do some work. But the American Bar Association notwithstanding, forwarding fees are in reality commissions for referring business.

So attractive are the prospects for forwarding fees that sometimes more than one lawyer will claim to be the forwarder in the same case.

"I've been caught in the middle of some real hassles over who was entitled to the forwarding fee," says one of New York's busiest bankruptcy lawyers.

"I'd get a call from one lawyer who says, 'I'm sending

over so and so. Remember, I'm the forwarder.'

"A couple of days later, I'll get a call from another lawyer who'll say, 'So and so has been my client for forty years and I sent him in to see you. Don't forget I'm the forwarder.'

"My response to this situation," he says, "is 'O.K., boys, there's only going to be one forwarding fee, and I don't care who the hell gets it. You two just work it out.' "

I asked another bankruptcy lawyer how he handles forwarding attorneys and he explained, "You know it's unethical to pay a forwarding fee unless the forwarding attorney does some work on the case. So we have him handle all the corporate work, getting up schedules from his client, investigative work, working up operating projections with the controller of the company. There's lots for him to do."

Then the attorney stopped and smiled. "You understand that's the theory. As a practical matter in most cases we never hear from the forwarding attorney except to discuss fees.

"There are, of course, cases in which the forwarder has a long-standing relationship with the client and he will remain active in the case because of a sincere interest in the client's welfare. But this is the exception rather than the rule."

Bankruptcy lawyers themselves are not cut off from the forwarding-fee gravy train. Here's how it's done, according to one of the pros:

An attorney has some experience in the bankruptcy field, but he doesn't have the reputation of a major bankruptcy firm, so he might not be able to get more than $5,000 for a fee. One of the majors might be able to get

$15,000 for the same case. So the forwarder still gets his $5,000 and he lets the big firms do all the work.

Also, there are some firms that handle only creditors' work. If they get a debtor, they can forward the case to one of the better known debtor's attorneys and come in for a piece of the fee.

Insolvencies which will require extensive court proceedings are also farmed out to the law firms that have the staff to handle that work.

"Why should I knock myself out running down to court and filing all those papers?" says one practitioner. "If I can put together a quick deal out of court, fine. Otherwise, I'll turn it over to another firm and just get the forwarding fee. I can make more money that way."

With the help of forwarding fees it's fairly easy to see where bankruptcy lawyers get their cases from—they get them from other lawyers. But there are other sources of business for the bankruptcy practitioners.

Carl Schaeffer, the out-of-court-settlement expert, says that he took very few cases from other lawyers because of the forwarding-fee problem.

"Most lawyers don't know the first thing about insolvency work, and if they tried to help me, they'd be more of a hindrance, so I refrained from taking many cases recommended by other lawyers."

Instead of relying on other lawyers, Schaeffer cultivated the friendship of credit men and accountants. He also developed a reputation for fair dealing.

A credit man for one of the major factoring firms describes his feelings about the great settlement negotiator like this: "There is only one Carl Schaeffer and I'm sorry he's not very active anymore. I had complete confidence in him and I would recommend him to any of my customers who were in financial trouble. I knew that the creditors would get a fair deal and so would the client."

Schaeffer couldn't be in more complete agreement. "I achieved a practical result. The client was able to stay in business and the creditors didn't get the usual screwing."

In addition to recommendations from credit men and the word of mouth in the trade, Schaeffer found that accountants were excellent sources of business.

"The accountant has a tremendous influence over his clients. Every month the client sits down with the accountant, they go over the figures and they exchange confidences. They may even do a little tax cheating together. This develops a very close relationship.

"I was the unofficial attorney for a half dozen of the leading accountants and never charged a fee. I don't charge fees for favors. I also stayed away from tax work and got all their recommendations."

Schaeffer's forte was representing debtors and pushing through settlements without having to go to court.

He got started in the business in 1929, a very good year for the insolvencies business. A couple of years later he went out on his own because the law firm he was with refused to put the name Schaeffer into the partnership title.

A product of New York's lower East Side and one of the most colorful members of the insolvencies fraternity, Schaeffer developed a passion for Africa and worked closely with the legendary Dr. Albert Schweitzer. He helped finance the jungle doctor's hospital and for many years bought a fish dinner every Friday night for the lepers in Dr. Schweitzer's colony. He also ran with the show-business crowd, serving as business manager for

Actors Studio, the acting alma mater of methodologists Shelley Winters, Paul Newman, Marilyn Monroe, Rod Steiger and others.

The biggest bankruptcy firm in New York is Levin & Weintraub, a firm started in 1933 by Harris Levin, who is still hyperactive and whose baby-pink complexion camouflages one of the toughest negotiators in the business. Back in the thirties life was rough for young lawyers, and Levin had to teach school and sell shoes on Saturdays. He was able to set up shop for himself because he had a cousin who was the credit manager for a food wholesaler and could fee him collection work.

With this as a nucleus, Benjamin Weintraub, a school chum, joined him, and from this start the firm soon became a dominant law firm representing creditors in the food field. They had a lock on just about every supermarket, restaurant and nightclub bust in New York, and for a time there were plenty of them—particularly restaurants and nightclubs. Levin says that bankruptcies in nightclubs were coming so quickly that at one point he was handling three separate nightclub corporations that had gone broke in the same location.

"The place went broke and somebody else opened it up and he went broke. Then a third corporation took it over and suffered the same fate."

As in any other field, fashions change in the bankruptcy business. TV killed nightclubs completely, so that source dried up for bankruptcies. Most food wholesalers disappeared with the growth of the huge supermarket chains, which bought directly from food processors and manufacturers. The trend toward chain-operated restaurants cut sharply into the volume of restaurant bankruptcies.

But over the years Levin & Weintraub's reputation in the insolvencies field grew, and as their old sources of bankruptcies petered out, newer and bigger ones came. It now does debtor work almost exclusively and its practice is pretty much confined to insolvencies. L & W's two principal competitors for debtor cases are Leinwand, Maron, Hendler & Krause and Levy, Levy & Ruback.

A good many of L & W's cases get to their offices on referrals from other lawyers, including some of the top Wall Street law firms.

Commercial finance companies are another good source of business for L & W and other bankruptcy practitioners. Finance companies are lenders of last resort—they will extend credit to companies that the banks won't touch with a ten-day note. The reason the finance companies can be so brave is that they lend against collateral, such as accounts receivable, inventory, machinery, real estate, etc.

They leave themselves enough of a cushion in the collateral so that even if the borrower goes broke, the liquidation of the security will provide enough cash to pay off the finance-company loan—plus legal expenses and interest charges.

And since the finance companies are willing to lend money to financially unstable concerns, their clients go bankrupt fairly frequently. Thus the finance companies are in a position to steer business down to the bankruptcy fraternity.

Lest I be accused of perpetuating another myth—namely that any company that gets tied up with a commercial finance company will surely go bankrupt—let me explain a bit further. A company that's slipping badly and must borrow from a finance company because no bank will extend credit will probably assure itself of bankruptcy because the higher interest cost will make it that much tougher to survive. However, finance companies also service growing companies that need more money than a bank is willing to lend, and the finance companies can cite a long list of major corporations that were able to grow because of the extra financing available from secured lenders.

The bankruptcy bar is in a position to reciprocate for finance-company-directed business. When a firm goes into Chapter XI, it usually needs interim financing to keep it operating until a plan can be worked out. While you might think that lending money to a company in bankruptcy proceedings is a form of financial masochism, this is not the case. Commercial finance companies can arrange to tie up enough assets and charge high enough rates to make this kind of business comfortable and profitable. The bankruptcy attorney can make the decision on what finance company will get a crack at the business.

Incidentally, if you'd like to pick up a couple of easy bucks, recommend a client to a commercial finance company. The usual deal will net the finder 5 percent of all charges earned on the recommended account for as long as it stays with the finance company.

Ethical considerations inhibit attorneys and accountants from accepting this type of finder's fee, but here again ethics sometimes take a back seat to greed.

Dealing with a businessman who has been running a large enterprise and suddenly finds himself in the office of a bankruptcy lawyer is a touchy task.

"Most of them are in a state of shock," says Levin. "It's a traumatic experience and it's up to me to nurse them along and restore their confidence. You really have to be on call twenty-four hours a day to minister to them. To start with, I give them a pep talk. I tell them about Ford and the three hundred million they lost on the Edsel; and du Pont and all the millions they blew on Corfam; and RCA and the five hundred million or so they lost in the computer business. The only reason they didn't go broke, I say, is that they're so big they could absorb those kind of losses. I tell them that everybody makes mistakes and that the world hasn't come to an end. I think my practice is fifty percent law and the other fifty percent the unlicensed practice of psychiatry," Levin concludes.

Not only does the debtor pose a serious psychological problem, but so do the creditors. One recurrent problem is the Cadillac syndrome.

"There must be something in the statute stating that everyone who files a Chapter XI petition or who goes into negotiation for a settlement must run a Cadillac or Lincoln," one bankruptcy lawyer says wearily. Nothing irritates a creditor as much as seeing someone who owes him money riding around in a shiny Caddy while the creditor is pushing a five-year-old Chevy.

"I had one case that almost blew apart because of the Cadillac syndrome. This debtor not only had a Cadillac but he had a chauffeur driving it. On the day of his creditors' meeting, he drives up with his Cadillac and has his chauffeur wait downstairs while he attends to the business of telling his creditors why he can't pay.

"Then when the meeting was over, in a gesture of good will, he tells the creditors that he has his car downstairs and was headed uptown and would anyone like a lift. Through it all he was completely oblivious of the slow burn the creditors were doing.

"I whisked him out of the room as quickly as I could and explained a few of the facts of life.

"'Shmuck,' I said, 'don't you realize that you owe those guys more than a million dollars and some of them may lose their big two-hundred-a-week jobs because they gave you credit? Now take that goddamned chauffeur and send him as far away from here as you can and get rid of the limousine too.'"

Worse than the ubiquitous Cadillac is the occasional yacht. Not too many bankrupts turn up with yachts, but it does happen. In a recent bankruptcy the owner of the company had a forty-five-foot yacht that cost $95,000. The boat was in the individual's name, but about $30,000 of the corporation's money had been used to keep up the payments on it. At the time of the bankruptcy, there was still some $40,000 due on the boat and the bank had a first lien against it. Chances are creditors will get nothing out of the boat except perhaps the satisfaction of having dealt with a bankrupt with class.

Notwithstanding all the talk of Cadillacs and yachts in the context of bankruptcy, the impression that people go into bankruptcy or Chapter XI to make money is a myth. The overwhelming majority of businessmen that go to their creditors either to work out a settlement or to throw in the sponge do so only in complete desperation.

One of my favorite bankruptcy stories illustrates the extremes to which a man will go to avoid bankruptcy. It seems there was this manufacturer who was a pillar of the community. He headed fund-raising committees, he made speeches at the trade-association meetings, he was friendly with the city's top politicians and he was justly proud of all his accomplishments.

But as luck would have it, he picked the wrong color and the wrong fabric and the wrong styles and he knew he was going broke.

The disgrace was too much to bear and he contemplated suicide as the only way out. Being a considerate man who wanted to make sure his family would have no problems, he saw that his insurance was in order and even went to a friend who was an undertaker to see that burial arrangements would be dignified and proper.

But when he told his story, the undertaker came up with a solution.

"Why kill yourself?" he asked. "I've known you for many years and I think you're too good a man to take your own life. Why not let me fix up a phony funeral for you? I can make you up, put you in the box, the whole thing—only you won't be dead. I'll give you something to slow down all your body functions and we'll invite all your creditors to the funeral and they'll all feel sorry for you and nobody will be the wiser. Then when it's over, you can go to another town and start a new life.

The desperate man was delighted with the idea and agreed to go along.

Came the day of the funeral and there he lay with his hands folded across his chest, surrounded by flowers, soft organ music playing, and one by one his creditors stepped up to the coffin for a final goodbye.

"Sam," said the first creditor, "why did you do it? You owed me a few thousand dollars, but what does it mean compared with friendship? You could have come to me and I'd wipe it out in a second. Sam, it was only money. Why didn't you come to me?"

The second creditor stepped up to the coffin and spoke

in the same vein. "Sam, my God, Sam, what did you do? For a few lousy bucks you were afraid to ask. Sam, you'll never know how much it hurt that you didn't think enough of our friendship to talk, to explain. Not only would I forget what you owed me, I'd have given you a blank check to start up again. Sam, you did a terrible thing to me."

But the next creditor took an entirely different attitude. "Sam, you sonofabitch. I trusted you. I gave you more credit than I could afford. Do you know that my entire capital was tied up in the goods I gave you and I'm going to have to close? My wife and kids don't have what to wear, the bank is going to foreclose on my house. Sam, I know you're dead, you bastard, but just for my own satisfaction I'm going to take this knife and stick it right into your heart and twist it around four times."

Whereupon Sam opens one eye and out of the corner of his mouth says, "*You* I'll pay."

Bankruptcy is a public announcement of failure, and the damage to the ego will offset whatever financial advantages bankruptcy offers.

Harris Levin complains that the reluctance of most troubled businessmen to take decisive action makes the lawyer's job more difficult.

"Usually when a business gets into trouble, the owner borrows from relatives, cashes in the kids' bonds, mortgages his house. He literally exhausts every possible source of funds.

"Then when he comes in to see me, he can't raise another dime. If I had that one hundred thousand or one hundred fifty thousand he borrowed and sank into the business, I could do a lot more for him in the way of putting through some kind of deal with his creditors. But too often it's too late by the time they come in to my office."

Ruben Schwartz, another attorney active in insolvencies, agrees that reluctance to go into a bankruptcy proceeding while there is still a chance to save the business is more of a problem than those looking for a quick killing at the expense of creditors. Schwartz's participation in insolvencies stems from the large number of clients he has in a bankruptcy-prone field. He represents about 500 women's sportswear manufacturers (about 150 on a regular retainer) and an assortment of other soft-goods firms. Women's sportswear is the kind of business that can be started up with very little capital ($20,000 used to be the standard initial investment, but inflation has pushed this figure up to about $50,000). With a $50,000 capital, they try to do a $1 million volume, which means they have to turn their capital twenty times a year—no easy task. It's no rarity for a client to go broke, and Schwartz handles the insolvency proceeding.

"My practice runs from the cradle to the grave," says Schwartz, who, in his middle fifties, has the build of a middleweight boxer and wears a tan that always looks fresh from a vacation in the Bahamas.

"I help to organize the businesses, look for mergers, take them public, handle their labor negotiations, even matrimonial problems, if they're not too complicated. And if they go broke, I try to work out the best deal I can for them."

He concurs in the opinion that clients in difficulty wait too long before taking the action needed to save the business.

"I have one client," says Schwartz, "who is losing

money in a terrible hurry, and there's not a chance in the world that he'll be able to avoid going broke. I told him that now is the time to file a Chapter XI petition, while he still has something.

"If he goes into Chapter XI now, he can freeze everybody, work down his overhead, get rid of any contracts he's hung up with and then offer his creditors a decent settlement. But if he waits until he's forced into it by judgments and liens and attachments, his business may never recover and he'll have nothing to offer his creditors.

"But he won't listen. He's got his pride and he's just going to knock himself out trying to stall off the inevitable."

Credit men, of course, are appalled at the thought of encouraging the filing of bankruptcy proceedings, but they do urge their customers to be more candid when trouble strikes, and if there is a valid reason for calling creditors together, they'll usually cooperate.

The art of extracting a fee from a man whose business is heading for oblivion is something you can never learn at law school, but the bankruptcy practitioners have been quite successful at it. Probably the most convincing argument is that an attorney's fee that comes out of a failing business doesn't cost the debtor anything because the money really belongs to creditors.

It is customary for the attorneys to take a fee before they begin working on a case. The lawyer who knows his business will insist on a certified check because experience has taught them that checks have a nasty way of bouncing when dealing with a busted client.

For one thing, just about the time a troubled businessman goes to see a bankruptcy lawyer, the bank could be getting ready to offset against the man's account.

Thus, while the company bank account shows a balance adequate to cover the lawyer's fee, by the time the check clears the bank could have closed out the account through its right of offset. Incidentally, one of the first steps a bankruptcy lawyer takes if his new client has money on deposit in a bank with a loan that could be offset is get the money into another bank.

"Don't take the money all out at once because that would arouse the bank's suspicion. Just draw it out a little at a time and make sure to leave a couple of hundred dollars in the account," the client is advised.

Bankruptcy lawyers tend to identify with the medical profession and consider themselves healers of sick businesses. The public identifies them more closely with undertaking. But both the doctor and the undertaker expect to be paid. In the case of ailing businesses, medical fees run higher than undertaking charges.

According to Stanley S. Horvath, a bankruptcy practitioner who learned the ropes through a long-time association with Carl Schaeffer, a small business that has to be liquidated in court proceedings will require an attorney's fee somewhere between $1,000 and $2,500 to get the legal wheels turning. But if the debtor wants to put through a deal with creditors to keep his business going, then the fee will start in the $3,500 to $5,000 range. "It all depends on the size and complexity of the case and how much work will be involved," says Horvath.

"Some attorneys won't even begin to discuss a debtor's problems without first being paid, but I like to find out just what's involved before requesting a fee. If I see that someone is there just to pick my brains, then I put a quick end to the conversation."

Just as doctors and undertakers have developed techniques for getting money out of people in times of extreme stress, so have the bankruptcy attorneys.

"It used to embarrass me to be dickering over payment with a man who's all shook up about his business falling apart, but after a couple of years you get used to it," says one veteran. "I tell him that creditors and the courts recognize the right of a debtor to be represented by counsel and for counsel to be paid for his services.

"Then if he says he can't pay you now but will pay later, I tell him that I know he's insolvent and that nobody else would give him credit with this knowledge, so why should I be expected to do what his other creditors won't do? I'm extending new services and I'm entitled to be paid. Then I point out that I'm not asking for the full fee, just a retainer. If the case is successful and I can put through a deal for him, then I'll ask for more. If no settlement can be made, then the retainer becomes my entire fee."

There's really no rule of thumb for determining fees. What it comes down to is that the fee is based on what the traffic will bear.

Specialization has a way of feeding on itself, and the trend is for professionals to concentrate on learning more and more about less and less. In the area of bankruptcy law, this trend has given rise to attorneys who represent only the creditors' side of a bankruptcy case and others who represent only debtors. There are two law firms that are so closely associated with the credit-granting community in the textile-apparel industry that they will not represent debtors.

The concept of representing only creditors is not new

and apparently grew out of the bankruptcy scandals of the late 1920s. A leading bankruptcy attorney of the period was C. Edward Benoit, who was called upon to do work for the Irving Trust Company. The bank had been appointed the standing receiver in New York because of all the hanky-panky surrounding a so-called bankruptcy ring. Benoit also was approached by an anti-fraud group composed of prominent textile-mill representatives and asked to work with them. He agreed to represent only creditors and in turn was assured of a continuing flow of business. Benoit died suddenly in 1932 when he was only thirty-nine years old, and the law firm now known as Hahn, Hessen, Margolis & Ryan fell heir to much of the Benoit practice.

Otterbourg, Steindler, Houston & Rosen is another law firm whose bankruptcy practice traces back to the days when the Irving Trust was standing receiver.

There are conflict-of-interest problems that arise in representing creditors one day and a debtor the next, particularly for attorneys whose practice is concentrated in a single industry. To avoid the possible conflict, Carl Schaeffer would represent only debtors. There are other firms that work both sides of the street, but generally their practice will be oriented in one direction or the other.

A striking exception to this pattern is the practice of Frederick E. M. Ballon, the founding partner of Ballon, Stoll & Itzler. Attorney Ballon not only represents creditors and debtors, but he will do it at the same time. In other words, he'll represent creditors in one case and while that case is still current he'll appear before those same creditors representing a debtor. He's even changed sides in midstream.

He had one case in which he was on the creditors' committee when the debtor decided that his own attorney was inadequate and asked Mr. Ballon to represent him. Mr. Ballon called the creditors' committee together and they agreed it would be all right for him to resign from the committee and go over and represent the debtor.

"I successfully consummated a settlement and kept the company on as a retainer client," Ballon says with obvious pride.

How is it possible to represent both sides in negotiations? How can a lawyer who meets with a group of creditors in the morning and tries to get his client, a financially ailing businessman, the best deal he can from the creditors turn around in the afternoon and try to get those same creditors top dollar from another debtor?

It's not easy. Some lawyers say it just can't be done, but Ballon has been doing it for years and with great financial success. As attorney for the creditors' committee in Grayson-Robinson Stores, a large women's-apparel chain that went into Chapter XI in 1962, he picked up a fee of $125,000, and a couple of years later as attorney for Miracle Mart, another chain that went into Chapter XI, he earned $160,000. Many of the same companies that were creditors of Grayson-Robinson were stuck in Miracle Mart.

The issue of sitting on both sides of the bankruptcy fence caused Ballon to split off from the establishment. Back in the 1930s he worked closely with the New York Credit Men's Adjustment Bureau in a drive to head off the rising flood of fraudulent bankruptcies. The Bureau is a membership corporation that was and is largely dominated by the factors and the major textile firms. Ballon recalls that in one case the Bureau's anti-fraud fund gave him a $100 check as a reward for pressing an investigation that resulted in the jailing of a crooked bankrupt.

But the Bureau, which contended that an attorney could be effective as a creditors' attorney only if he did not represent debtors, objected to Ballon's flexible attitude. As far as the Bureau was concerned, he would have to limit his practice to creditor work.

But Ballon says he was not prepared to let any organization "dictate to an attorney as to who his clients should be," and he broke with the Bureau.

He rationalizes his ability to work either end this way: "I can look at a set of figures in an insolvency case, analyze them and in two hours I'll know the case should be settled for X percent—give or take a point or two. Within a small tolerance there is really only one good settlement, so it doesn't make any difference which side of the fence I'm on."

He says that his experience on both sides makes him better able to do the right thing. "If I represent a debtor and give the creditors a bad deal, they'll never deal with me again. And if I don't get a fair settlement for the debtors I represent, I won't get many debtors' cases sent to me."

As it now stands, Ballon says he gets much of his insolvency work through recommendations from people who've dealt with him in negotiations either with him or against him.

Ballon started practicing law in the negligence field, but through a family connection he worked his way into insolvencies.

His father was a silk converter (a converter buys fabric

in the greige or unfinished state and then has it dyed and converted into a product that can be used to manufacture apparel, drapes or whatever). His father's firm was Century Factors' largest client, so Century's insolvency work went to young Ballon. Also, many of Ballon Senior's customers and suppliers found their way into his son's law office.

Today Ballon's law firm gets about one third of its income from insolvency-related work and the rest from a general corporate practice.

For a law firm to restrict itself to representing creditors only it needs a solid power base for generating this kind of business. Both Hahn, Hessen, Margolis & Ryan, and Otterbourg, Steindler, Houston & Rosen have it.

Among the firms that regularly give insolvency work to HHM & R are James Talcott, Inc., Burlington Industries, J. P. Stevens & Company and John P. Maguire & Company. These four do a combined volume of $5 billion or so and naturally generate millions in bad debts. If there's a creditors' meeting and Talcott, Burlington and Stevens are among the major creditors, it's not too difficult to guess what law firm will be elected counsel for the creditors' committee.

OSH & R also has a formidable array of clients that provide insolvency work to that office, the most important of which are Meinhard-Commercial Corporation and William Iselin & Company. Meinhard and Iselin are factoring subsidiaries of CIT Financial Corporation and together do a volume in the neighborhood of $2 billion.

Although strong competitive spirit motivates these two law firms, when an insolvency case is big enough and the power balanced out so neither is dominant, they will swallow their animosity and serve as co-counsel, splitting the fee.

The fees for creditor work, particularly in out-of-court-settlement cases, are most attractive. The paperwork is minimal and the cases can often be cleaned up in a matter of weeks rather than the months or years that are needed to drag a proceeding through the courts; the fees are controlled by committee members rather than by referees or judges, and they're not a matter of public record, as are court-approved fees. Furthermore, committee members who approve the attorneys' fees are the same people who put the attorney in the case in the first place, so they're inclined to be friendly.

One attorney who handles mostly debtors and takes most of his cases into court says with a touch of envy in his voice, "I think some of those fellows [creditors' attorneys] get a thousand dollars an hour in a clean out-of-court deal. What do they have to do? They show up at two meetings for a couple of hours, make a few phone calls, draw up an agreement that is usually no different from thousands they've drawn up before. They tell a secretary to pull form number four from the file and they just fill in the blanks. In all, they probably put in five hours' work, and a five-thousand-dollar fee for that kind of case isn't at all unusual."

The creditors' specialists disagree violently and maintain that they earn their fees because of their profound knowledge of the law and get so many cases because they do their job so well.

Creditor-oriented law firms are content to turn down debtor business that might come their way because they don't want to jeopardize their creditor business.

Conrad B. Duberstein joined OSH & R in 1971 after about thirty years of practicing insolvency law on both sides. Now he can't represent debtors that have any link to the textile industry because of OSH & R's other clients.

"OSH and R must preserve its image as creditor representatives," he says. However, in a field such as electronics, where Mr. Duberstein has strong ties from his earlier law practice, he can accept and handle debtor cases. Mr. Duberstein, one of the most personable of the bankruptcy bar members (he sings opera with Referee Babitt at parties), has actually been involved in the business since 1932, when he was sixteen and a half years old. At that time he dropped out of school and went to work for his uncle, Samuel C. Duberstein, one of Brooklyn's leading bankruptcy referees.

"I became an expert in bankruptcy long before I became a lawyer," he says.

One of the top bankruptcy practitioners in New York and one of the nation's leading authorities on bankruptcy law is Charles Seligson, who at seventy still holds a full professorship at New York University and continues an active insolvencies practice.

He literally wrote the book on bankruptcy law and is currently working with other experts on a plan for a complete overhaul of the bankruptcy laws. When in 1971 Secretary of the Treasury John B. Connally was seeking Congressional approval for a $250 million Government-guaranteed bank loan to save Lockheed from possible bankruptcy, Professor Seligson was called to testify as an expert witness. He told the legislators that it would be disastrous if the company was forced into the bankruptcy courts. He said that the cash flow needed to keep Lockheed operating was so huge that it could be forced to shut down in any reorganization proceeding under the Bankruptcy Act, thus adding thousands to California's already bulging unemployment rolls. Lockheed got the loan.

Professor Seligson came to New York from Raleigh, North Carolina, in the 1920s and went to work for a credit insurance company. During the 1930s the Irving Trust Company used him as their attorney in some of their small cases. The classic approach for developing a reputation in those days was to work hard trying to put crooked bankrupts behind bars. He did such a good job that when the father-in-law of one of the bankrupts Seligson put in jail needed a lawyer, the prisoner recommended Seligson.

And now, instead of the small Irving Trust cases, Seligson gets appointments from the Federal judges in major cases—and chances are he'll turn them down at this stage.

7 Through the Swinging Courtroom Doors

In 1971 there were about 180,000 individual, nonbusiness bankruptcies filed, representing an increase of more than 1700 percent over a twenty-five-year period. Losses to creditors from consumer bankruptcies are running in the neighborhood of $1 billion a year.

With this kind of volume, it's apparent that the courts can't spend much time with each case.

Routine filings are handled on an assembly-line basis. The bankrupts are run through the judicial process with about the same attention given prostitutes and street peddlers. There are exceptions when a bankrupt shows up with some money in his estate, but these are rare.

Bankruptcy courts have been a haven for the famous and the obscure. Actor Mickey Rooney is no stranger to bankruptcy. Singer Eddie Fisher filed a bankruptcy petition in Puerto Rico, showing debts of nearly $1 million and something like $40,000 in assets. That same year, 1971, Dick Haymes, a singer who made it big during the late Thirties with the Jimmy Dorsey orchestra, picked London for his bankruptcy. (It's a good idea to file your

bankruptcy as far away from your creditors as possible.)
Haymes claimed he blew $2 million on his onetime wife
Rita Hayworth. Vic Damone made it a trio of singers by
filing for bankruptcy shortly after Fisher and Haymes.
Appropriately enough, Damone filed his petition in Las
Vegas.

Back in 1948 showman Mike Todd went into bankruptcy, but some embarrassing questions came up and he
agreed to waive his discharge. Instead he bought up all
the creditors' claims against him for a fraction of their
face value and then promised that if he ever made a big
hit again, he'd pay off every cent. Subsequently he made a
new fortune as producer of the movie *Around the World
in 80 Days* but died in a plane crash in 1958 before
making good on his promise.

These are the cases that get in the papers. But the great
bulk of bankruptcies are more like the young secretary
from Manhattan.

She had a fairly good job, earning $7,000 a year, and
ran up an assortment of debts at some of New York City's
finest department stores and banks totaling $8,000. She
couldn't pay off that kind of debt load, so she filed for
bankruptcy.

Her list of creditors showed $132 owing to Bonwit
Teller, $145 to Saks Fifth Avenue, $244 to Macy's, $500 to
Unicard, $690 to BankAmericard, $197 to B. Altman &
Company, another $170 to Arnold Constable, about $800
to Gimbels, $140 to Bloomingdale's, $1,375 to Beneficial
Finance and another $3,000 to Bankers Trust Company.

Nobody showed up at her first meeting of creditors.
The referee asked her what she had bought with all that
money and she said, "Clothing." She walked out of the
courtroom ready to start fresh.

For an attorney's fee of $350 and a $50 filing fee she had bought herself $8,000 worth of clothes. Not a bad deal.

An individual bankrupt with no assets—the overwhelming majority have none, or at least don't show any—must make just one appearance in court. This is for the so-called first meeting of creditors. The purpose of the meeting is to give creditors an opportunity to question the bankrupt and to elect a trustee and a creditors' committee.

But if there are no assets, there's no need for a trustee and it's a waste of time for creditors to show up because there's nothing in it for them. Thus the first meeting of creditors turns out to be a meeting of the bankrupt, his attorney and the Referee in Bankruptcy.

Referees, being human, differ in their attitudes toward the bankrupts who appear before them. Some think the bankrupts are just a bunch of poor slobs who got caught up in a credit-card society that virtually forced them to buy more than they could reasonably be expected to pay for. Others view bankrupts as irresponsible or dishonest individuals who should be made to sweat.

With these differing attitudes, referees vary in their styles of handling the stream of bankrupts that appear before them. Some ask a few perfunctory questions and get through thirty or forty first meetings in an hour or two. Others take more time trying to make the bankrupts squirm.

I remember one referee who would pick a bankrupt, apparently at random, and subject him to a merciless third-degree.

"What did you do with your money? Didn't you know when you bought all this merchandise that you couldn't pay for it? Where are your records? Did you make any preferential payments?"

This would go on for fifteen minutes or so, and the poor bastard would leave the witness stand covered with perspiration and relieved that the referee didn't send him to jail for life.

Meantime the rest of the bankrupts would sit by in horror, awaiting their turn under the gun. The attorneys who knew the whole charade sat impatiently, hoping he'd get finished already so they could go to their next hearing.

After raking one unfortunate over the coals, the referee would run the rest through with just a couple of questions.

Generally, referees try to find a middle course. They want to impress an individual that bankruptcy is not to be taken lightly. At the same time, they don't want to humiliate the bankrupt or make him feel like a criminal.

Referee Asa S. Herzog of New York's Southern District, a national figure in the bankruptcy scene (he's one of the few referees who were practicing bankruptcy lawyers before their appointment to the bench), puts it this way: "Bankruptcy is a serious business, and the bankrupt should have the feeling of coming into a courtroom and shivering a bit about it. A man in a black robe questions him. He should not be made to feel degraded or disgraced, but he should be made aware that he did something with his life that is serious. A judicial flavor must be retained. They come in here and they shake and that's how it should be."

Referee Herzog makes it a practice to ask each bankrupt if he has any credit cards. If the bankrupt has any, he must surrender them on the spot. Credit cards could lead to their downfall again, the referee warns. "Buy for cash," he says.

Another New York referee, Roy Babitt, tries to schedule two or three first meetings on one day's calendar and plans them so the individual bankrupt gets to hear some complex legal arguments in a commercial bankruptcy case. This is designed to emphasize the judicial nature of the bankruptcy proceeding.

"If a referee schedules twenty or thirty consecutive first meetings," says Referee Babitt, "each watches the other and sees it's really nothing. The proceedings are degraded and the bankrupt leaves unimpressed."

A routine first meeting goes something like this: The bankrupt swears to tell the whole truth and takes the witness stand. The referee then asks the witness if he signed his schedules and statement of affairs (the papers showing the bankrupt's assets, liabilities, creditors and other background and financial information) and if the information contained therein is true. The witness says yes. The referee briefly scans the papers to see if there are any assets that would require a trustee. If there are no assets, he sends the bankrupt home.

That's the whole deal. In a month or so, the bankrupt receives his discharge, which relieves him of almost all debts incurred prior to the filing of the bankruptcy petition.

Creditors are advised by mail of the bankrupt's discharge with the following legal notice:

Notice is hereby given of entry on [date] of an order of discharge which has become final and which releases the above-named person, adjudged a bankrupt on a petition filed on [date of filing] from all dischargeable debts and declares any judgment theretofore or thereafter obtained in any court null and void as a determination of personal liability of the bankrupt. . . . The said order of discharge enjoins all creditors whose debts are discharged from instituting or continuing any action or employing any process to collect such debts as personal liabilities of the bankrupt above named.

Some debts are not dischargeable. Taxes have to be paid in full, unless you can make a deal with the Internal Revenue Service. If you owe a bundle in taxes, the only thing bankruptcy will do for you is clean up your other debts so you can concentrate on paying your taxes. Alimony and support payments are also nondischargeable, as are debts created through willful and malicious personal injury. Credit obtained by fraud cannot be wiped out by a bankruptcy discharge.

Bankruptcy referees who handle hundreds of cases every year are in substantial agreement that easy credit, changing public attitudes toward debt and the failure by creditors to follow up once a customer goes into bankruptcy are at the root of the mushrooming bankruptcy rate.

"Nobody seems to give a shit" was the unjudicial explanation of one referee. "In case after case, nobody shows up and then they complain that they never see a dime in bankruptcy cases.

"I know damn well that in many of these cases the bankrupt knows when he bought all that stuff that there wasn't a chance in the world that he would pay for it. That's fraud, but we don't have the power to do anything about it. Unless a creditor comes in and raises an objection, we have to give them their discharge. Apparently it doesn't pay the retailers to come. It's cheaper just to write off the bad debts.

"So I just ask the bankrupt a few questions: Do you have any bank accounts, any furs, any jewelry, any stocks or bonds? And always get the same answer: 'No, Your Honor.'"

The only creditors who do occasionally raise a fuss are the small-loan companies and some banks, and in this group some referees think these creditors go to the other extreme—harassing bankrupts with arbitrary charges and using various ruses to collect on discharged debts.

The prevalence of post-discharge harassment led to a recent change in the law to eliminate the abuse.

It had been a fairly widespread practice for persistent creditors to sue in state courts on debts that had been wiped out in bankruptcy. The suits were often initiated with sewer service—the debtor never knew he was being sued until he discovered there was a judgment against him and his salary was being attached. An unsophisticated debtor wouldn't know how to cope with these fancy legal maneuvers and would find that his bankruptcy discharge was a meaningless piece of paper.

In November of 1970 the Federal bankruptcy courts were given sole jurisdiction in suits against bankrupts involving debts predating bankruptcy.

Another ploy used by creditors prior to the November law change was to go into state court and claim a particular debt was not dischargeable, and if the state court agreed the creditor could go ahead with a judgment and grab whatever assets he could lay his hands on. Under the new law only the bankruptcy courts can decide whether or not a debt is dischargeable.

Once a person gets a discharge, the bankruptcy route is closed to him for the next six years. There are reports that some merchants prey on freshly discharged bankrupts, actively seeking to sell them on credit. Since these customers can't go bankrupt again for a while, the theory goes, they are sure to pay new bills.

I think this is more myth than reality. Most merchants prefer to steer clear of a freshly discharged bankrupt. The problem for a bankrupt is getting credit, not avoiding it.

Bankruptcy proceedings cannot impair the right of anyone holding a mortgage on a debtor's property, but there is the possibility of some reforms in this area.

Referee Herzog points out that a discharge doesn't do any good when "the man from the bank takes the car and house away, the furniture store repossesses the living-room suite, and the appliance store takes away the refrigerator and the television set."

Combining some of the features of straight bankruptcy with some aspects of Chapter XIII (wage-earners plan) might produce an equitable solution, according to the referee.

"Let the bankrupt obtain a discharge covering his dischargeable debts and then set up a payment plan for secured creditors. The secured creditors would be paid off by a weekly deduction from the debtor's wages.

"This would help rehabilitate the debtor and at the same time get the secured creditors paid off. There might also be a fresh appraisal of the security at the time of the bankruptcy to establish the real value of the security. Why should a debtor have to pay off a nine-hundred-dollar balance on a car that's only worth five hundred dollars?"

In order to declare bankruptcy you must turn over all your assets to the court to be distributed among your creditors. However, some assets can be retained. Exemptions vary from state to state, but generally a bankrupt can keep the tools of his trade (a plumber can keep his wrenches, a writer his typewriter), household furniture, clothes, insurance and, in some states, his home. In New York there is no exemption for a home, while in Texas the homestead exemption is so liberal that a person could go bankrupt and still keep a half-million-dollar mansion.

Jewelry and automobiles should be turned in, but this is really a matter of discretion.

"If a man has a watch, I'm not going to take it away from him, or if he has a ten-year-old Plymouth, I'll let him keep that too," says one referee. "One man, I recall, needed his car to get to work. It would have been a crime to force him to turn it over to a trustee."

A sore point in bankruptcy administration is the filing fee. It seems absurd to force a person to pay a fee to have himself declared legally broke, but such is the case.

It costs a minimum of $50 to go bankrupt. This includes a $37 filing fee, a $3 clerk's fee and $10 to cover the cost of a trustee if there are no assets in the estate to compensate him. If no trustee is appointed, the $10 is returned to the bankrupt.

The $50 is supposed to be paid at the time the bankruptcy petition is filed, but there are provisions for extensions up to nine months to complete the payment. But there's one catch: Until the fee is paid, the bankrupt can't get his discharge. That is, if he doesn't pay the fee, he can't get his debts wiped out.

In addition to the filing fee, there is the cost of an

attorney. There's no requirement that a lawyer be used, but few prospective bankrupts know enough to file a do-it-yourself petition. The prevailing rate in 1972 was between $250 and $350 for the standard individual petition.

The amount of the lawyer's fee is disclosed in the petition so the referee has a chance to review it. If he thinks an attorney is taking advantage of a client by charging too much, the court has the power to force the attorney to refund part of it. It's not unusual for a referee to bawl out a lawyer before a packed courtroom for taking too much money from a client.

Although there is no fixed minimum on how much a person must owe to be eligible for bankruptcy, it doesn't make sense for anyone who owes less than $500. After all, a bankruptcy must be profitable.

There has been much litigation over the filing-fee question, and a series of apparently contradictory decisions has left the whole subject up in the air.

In September of 1971 Federal Judge Anthony J. Travia in Brooklyn Federal Court ruled: "The statutory requirements of prepayment of a filing fee to obtain a discharge violate his [the petitioner's] Fifth Amendment right to due process, including equal protection."

A month later Referee Babitt, in another case, held that the filing-fee requirement for an indigent person did not violate any Constitutional rights.

Referee Babitt found his case to be different factually from the Brooklyn action. In Brooklyn, the court clerk refused to accept the petition without prepayment of the fee, while in the Manhattan case the clerk accepted the petition and it was referred to Referee Babitt for a ruling on the filing-fee issue.

Referee Babitt, in a scholarly decision (referees' decisions contain all the accouterments of the judicial calling and are replete with case citations, footnotes and strange Latin phrases), ruled that although he sympathized with the bankrupt before him—a welfare recipient getting $53 a week—there was no violation of due process.

"In the case at bar," Referee Babitt wrote, "the requirements of fair play are satisfied, it seems to me, when the sole beneficiary of the judicial process that makes up the administration of bankruptcy is asked, under the most lenient terms authorized by the Supreme Court, to help bear the expense of that process which rehabilitates him. That that price lies more heavily on him does not constitute such discrimination on account of financial situation as to outrage the court's sense of justice in the context of the bankruptcy process."

He then went on to deny the application for a waiver of the fee and gave the bankrupt six months to pay the $50, with the provision for an extra three-month extension if required.

Later in the same month Referee Beryl E. McGuire in Buffalo, New York, ruled that the $50 filing-fee requirement was unconstitutional when applied to the very poor.

Referee McGuire held that while bankruptcy may not be a fundamental right, it's unconstitutional to withhold the privilege from anyone just because he's too poor to pay the $50 court fee.

So either the filing fee is Constitutional or it's unconstitutional. At this writing, Judge Travia's case is up for review before the United States Supreme Court, and the mess may be unscrambled there.

History is full of horror stories about the treatment of

debtors and the inhuman conditions in debtors' prisons. In ancient Greece (623 B.C.) debt was classified as a crime comparable to murder. Later the Greeks modified their laws and merely required debtors to sell their children as slaves and do mandatory service on creditors' land. Under Roman law, a borrower pledged himself as collateral, and if he didn't pay, the creditor had a choice of selling, killing or enslaving the debtor. Hindu law permitted a creditor to kill or maim a debtor, or, if the creditor was squeamish, just force the debtor to work for him.

In eighteenth-century England, a Parliamentary investigation of debtors' prisons found that jailers lived on what they could extort from prisoners and sometimes tortured them to death in overenthusiastic extortion efforts. General James Oglethorpe, who induced Parliament to conduct the investigation, established the colony of Georgia in 1732 as a debtors' refuge.

Colonial America was no better than England in the treatment of debtors. Debtors' prisons were dismal places. There were no beds and the food was at the barest subsistence level. Prisoners were whipped, branded and generally abused.

Debtors' prisons in the United States were abolished on a state-by-state basis. Kentucky ended the practice of imprisonment for debt in 1821 and was the first state to make the move. By the Civil War the rest of the states had followed.

We've come a long way from the days when debt was considered a crime and debtors were treated as criminals. Yet even today imprisonment for debt exists.

There is, of course, alimony jail, where husbands and ex-husbands who fall behind in their support payments can be put away indefinitely.

There is also a parallel in the bankruptcy field. If a debtor fails to comply with an order of the court to produce records or appear for examination or turn over assets, he can be cited for contempt, arrested and imprisoned until he purges himself of the contempt.

Usually a contempt order arises when the bankruptcy trustee can show that the bankrupt has concealed assets. Prior to World War II, all that had to be shown was that at one time the bankrupt had certain assets, and if he couldn't prove that he no longer had them, possession was presumed. If he was ordered to turn over the property or cash proceeds and he failed to comply, he'd be held in contempt and jailed.

The stock explanation in bankruptcy for money that seems to have disappeared is "I lost it at the races." Go prove that he didn't.

And a trustee's lawyer tries to do just that. He'll ask some basic questions about racing terms that any horse player should know. "What's the difference between win, place and show?" That's an easy one, and no bankrupt smart enough to secrete assets would have any trouble answering that. Then the questions get more specific: "What tracks did you go to?" That's another easy one and he'll probably rattle off the names of three or four.

"What horses did you bet on?"

"I don't remember."

"How much did you lose at one time?"

"I don't remember."

"Who was with you when you went to the track?"

"I don't remember."

On the basis of this kind of testimony a referee would probably decide the man was lying and certify him in contempt.

But if the bankrupt can prove he lost his money at the track, he's off the hook. There's nothing creditors can do.

I recall one bankrupt who claimed to have lost a fortune of his creditors' money at the races, and all they could do was fume and froth. He had thousands in canceled checks that had been cashed at the track.

He also was a former owner or part owner of several race horses, and to top it all, before his business had gone sour, some of his creditors were his guests at the track.

When he said he lost money at the races, who could say he hadn't?

In a contempt case, the debtor must stay in jail until he comes across with the assets or is able to convince the referee that he really can't comply. The theory holds that the prisoner has the key to his cell, and all he has to do to open the door is to comply with the order.

Some have stayed in jail for as long as twenty months before the court decided that if the prisoner actually had the key he would have used it.

To avoid having to wait over a year and a half to find out if a debtor was really holding out, more recent decisions require convincing proof of possession. The trustee must prove that the debtor had possession of the disputed assets at a recent point in time, or there's no case.

In addition to the turnover cases, failure to appear for examination can also result in imprisonment for contempt. Of course there's always the problem of finding someone who skips out on an examination, but if he can be located, he can be put away.

Not long ago a bankrupt spent four months in jail because he didn't show up for a hearing at which he was to be examined by the attorney for a small-loan company. The referee handling the case certified the bankrupt in contempt, a Federal judge issued an order and the man was picked up.

"The poor bastard sat in the can and nobody helped him," the referee explained later. "Not Legal Aid, nobody. Finally I got wind of it and I called an attorney who got him out. He was just a poor shnook who didn't do anything wrong. He was probably scared to death when he was served with this piece of paper, so he just tore it up, threw it away and hoped nothing would come of it."

When did I say debtors' prison was abolished?

If you're in business and you need help, you go to Chapter X or Chapter XI. If you're a wage earner but have been spending more than you earn, when things get out of hand you can file under Chapter XIII. You can then arrange to pay your debts over an extended period of time. Or you can just file a straight bankruptcy and not have to pay anyone anything anytime.

Some bankruptcy experts think Chapter XIII is just plain dumb, and in New York, where you find the most sophisticated bankruptcy people, you see very few of XIIIs. Why beat your brains out to pay off a lot of debts if you can get your debts expunged forever by getting a discharge in bankruptcy?

In certain areas of the country, notably in the South and parts of New England, Chapter XIII is very popular. Part of this popularity stems from the pride of individuals who want to pay off every cent they owe and part is the result of local pressures. Threats of a creditless existence for all eternity could turn a prospective bankrupt into the loving arms of Chapter XIII.

Currently, filings of Chapter XIII petitions are running at about 30,000 a year and account for 15 percent of all bankruptcies filed. It is a proceeding based on the Puritan ethic and highly regarded by square America. If you like Lawrence Welk, you'll love Chapter XIII.

Chapter XIII was included in the Chandler Act of 1938 when the Bankruptcy Act was revised and Chapter X and Chapter XI were born. But it took an article by the *Reader's Digest* in 1961, called "Ready Help for People in Debt," really to put Chapter XIII across. It is still known in some circles as the *Reader's Digest* chapter.

Essentially, the Chapter XIII proceeding involves a plan to pay creditors out over a period of time. The debtor makes periodic payments to a court-appointed trustee, who in turn distributes the money to creditors—after taking down 5 percent for himself.

The system is disturbingly similar to the debt-pooling plans under which many a distressed debtor was just shoved down deeper in his financial quagmire. There were and are legitimate nonprofit agencies that help a debt-burdened consumer dig himself out by counseling him on budgets and arranging for extra time on outstanding debts. Others have been set up just to take another bite out of some poor debtor's behind.

The debt-pooling business has an unsavory reputation. There was one in New York I remember that was put out of business by the Attorney General because of its sharpster operating methods.

The basic flaw in the debt-pooling concept is that

anyone in financial trouble who signs up with an agency immediately increases his debt. This is like giving a drowning man a drink of water.

The New York outfit I mentioned charged their clients 10 percent of the total debt. Someone who owed $1,000 when he walked in got a lot of smooth talk, but when he walked out he owed $1,100. Then when his payments started, the first hundred went to pay off the agency. Often by the time the agency fee was paid, the plan fell apart and the poor client was right back where he started —only poorer.

As far as the bankruptcy courts in New York are concerned, Chapter XIII might just as well not have happened. In fiscal 1971, out of 1,208 bankruptcy proceedings started in New York's Southern District, a grand total of six were Chapter XIIIs.

The New York referees just don't push it. "I'm not against Chapter XIII per se, but I'm against shoving it down people's throats," says one referee. "It has to be a voluntary action. In some areas people have just been sold a bill of goods.

"It's O.K. for social services to sell the concept, but I'm a judicial officer, not a social service worker, and it's often impractical. Suppose a guy is making thirteen thousand dollars or even fifteen thousand dollars a year and he owes one hundred thousand dollars. Forget it. He's never going to be able to pay that off in XIII. Or a guy taking home a hundred bucks a week and he has a couple of kids. He'd be nuts to file a XIII."

Another referee thinks Chapter XIII is a "form of peonage" and feels that many people who file under Chapter XIII are ill-advised.

The proceedings are also regarded as administrative monstrosities. The cases can run for seven or eight years, and the referees are married to them for all that time.

There is a move afoot to remove Chapter XIII proceedings from the bankruptcy courts and turn them over to a social-service agency. This would make some referees happy and is in tune with increasing emphasis on debt as a social problem rather than a legal one.

8 Arrangement or Reorganization

If you ever have had a tendency to confuse Chapter X and Chapter XI, here's all you have to remember. Chapter X is a petition for a reorganization and Chapter XI is a petition for an arrangement. This isn't going to help you understand the difference, but if someone should ask, just give him that answer. Chances are he'll listen carefully, nod knowingly and never go any further for fear of appearing obtuse.

But since this is going to be an honest presentation, we won't cop out.

Chapter XI was born with the Chandler Act of 1938, and one of the major innovations was to remove the stigma of "bankruptcy" from the company that filed under this section. Instead of being called a bankrupt, the company would be referred to as "debtor."

What the Chandler Act neglected to do was tell the newspapers about it. As far as the nation's press was concerned, a company that went into Chapter XI "filed for bankruptcy." With the passing of the years, the term "debtor" just didn't catch on, at least not outside the court proceedings themselves.

But debtor or bankrupt, Chapter XI is aimed at giving a troubled business a breathing spell—free of judgments, lawsuits, attachments, threatening phone calls and all the other harassments that beset a company with past-due bills. Chapter XI should be used only for companies that have some chance of survival; the hopeless cases should be directed into straight bankruptcy. But hope is an irrational emotion, and so a good percentage of Chapter XI cases ultimately end in bankruptcy.

The filing of a Chapter XI petition freezes all debts as of the date of the filing and in effect sets up a new company called the debtor-in-possession. The DIP has all the assets but none of the liabilities of the old company and so is able to go out and get new merchandise and keep going. New creditors are on a par with attorneys' fees, so they stand a good chance of getting paid.

Meanwhile, the old creditors are held up from collecting pre-filing debts and the company has time to locate and eliminate the causes of its problems, try to get a new financing and work out a plan to pay off the old creditors. If nothing can be done within a reasonable period (sometimes a company stays in Chapter XI proceedings for years) the business is liquidated, and if there's anything left after paying administration expenses and priorities, it goes out to creditors.

The "arrangement" I spoke of earlier is the plan finally arrived at and approved by the court and creditors to clean up the old indebtedness. It's usually a simple extension or settlement or a little bit of each. Say, full payment over a period of years, or 20 percent cash or 50 percent in installments—something along these lines. Sometimes the plans get fancy, offering various classes of stock and debentures and profit-sharing formulas.

Chapter X is also a product of the Chandler Act, and it offers the same protection against creditor harassment as Chapter XI. But it is designed to take care of the sweeping reorganization needed by a company with public stockholders, various classes of bondholders and a generally complicated financial structure. The difference is procedural rather than substantive.

In Chapter X the court appoints a trustee, who is assigned the task of running the business and finding a viable plan of reorganization, with the court and the Securities and Exchange Commission looking over his shoulder.

Much of the confusion over Chapter X and Chapter XI arises from a tendency to accept a false syllogism: Since Chapter X reorganization is for large companies with public ownership, ergo all large public companies that are driven into the bankruptcy courts must choose Chapter X.

The fact is, Chapter XI can be and has been used frequently and successfully by large public companies with major financial problems. Chapter X reorganization is avoided like some dread disease, and any bankruptcy lawyer with more than twenty minutes' experience in the business will fight fiercely to keep a client in Chapter XI rather than be forced into X.

There are a number of reasons for preferring XI over X, some altruistic and others pure selfishness. In the balance, it adds up to enlightened self-interest.

The legal guidelines for determining whether a large public company chooses X or XI have to do with the complexity of the relief required. The courts have ruled that if all a company needs to straighten itself out is a simple settlement of unsecured debt, then it can go through Chapter XI. But if the business requires a massive reorganization with changes in stockholders' rights and complete recapitalization, Chapter X is the place.

Bullfeathers! It's possible and practical to use Chapter XI and put through the most far-reaching changes, bring in new ownership, issue new classes of stock, convert stock to debt or debt to stock.

The principal obstacle to a public company's use of Chapter XI is the Securities and Exchange Commission. As the guardian of the public interest, the SEC may take the initiative to force a company that chose Chapter XI to transfer the proceedings into Chapter X. The SEC is a major participant in any Chapter X case, reviewing reorganizations proposed and being responsible for an investigation of the circumstances leading to the financial disaster. The SEC is charged with the responsibility of seeing that the public stockholders and bondholders are treated fairly.

Until August of 1962 when Grayson-Robinson Stores, Inc., filed a Chapter XI petition, the SEC had things pretty much its own way. Whenever a company with public shareholders filed an XI, the SEC would move to have it dismissed and transferred to X, and the courts almost invariably went along with the SEC.

Grayson-Robinson was a natural for Chapter X. It was a large corporation with sales of around $100 million a year, it had several thousand public stockholders, its stock was traded on the New York Stock Exchange, it had public bondholders and its snarled finances obviously required more than a simple settlement or extension of unsecured debts. But the company, or rather its attorneys, chose to file under Chapter XI.

The SEC moved in to force the proceedings into Chapter X, was defeated in the U.S. District Court and again in the Court of Appeals. The SEC then asked the Solicitor General to carry the case to the Supreme Court but was turned down. The basic argument of the attorneys for Grayson-Robinson (Paul, Weiss, Rifkind, Wharton & Garrison, a top firm reputed at the time to have strong ties with the Kennedy Administration) was that Chapter X would mean certain liquidation, while in Chapter XI there was a chance to revive the company. Grayson-Robinson's creditors supported the company's position. A Chapter XI plan was worked out which provided for full payment over ten years. Unfortunately for the proponents of Chapter XI, just about a year after the plan went through and before a single payment was made to creditors, Grayson-Robinson went into a straight bankruptcy.

For their efforts in putting through the Chapter XI plan—and it was an extremely complicated and difficult proceeding—Paul, Weiss, Rifkind was awarded a $265,000 fee; Frederick E. M. Ballon, as attorney for the creditors' committee, got $125,000; and S. D. Leidesdorf & Company, accountants, got $135,000.

Now, ten years after the original filing, the Grayson-Robinson bankruptcy case is finally being wound up and a brand-new set of fees are being awarded. Frederick E. M. Ballon, attorney for the trustee, has applied for a $400,000 fee, and the trustee, National Apparel Adjustment Council, is asking for $51,825.

The case of Grayson-Robinson plus developments in the stock market in the past decade have apparently cooled the SEC's zeal in pushing arrangement proceedings into reorganizations.

With the stock-market boom of 1967–68 and the bust of 1969–70, bankruptcy attorneys feel the SEC has become so overwhelmed with work it doesn't have the time or the manpower to chase after more bankruptcy work.

Whatever the reason, more and more companies with public stockholders are taking the Chapter XI route without SEC interference.

Chapter X reorganizations attract lawyers from all over the lot—not just the members of the bankruptcy club. This is because any lawyer who makes a "contribution" to the plan that is confirmed, or makes a contribution that is beneficial to the administration of the estate, or even a lawyer who comes up with a meritorious objection to the confirmation of a plan of reorganization, is entitled to "reasonable compensation" for his services.

Thus most Chapter X hearings are crawling with lawyers representing creditors, stockholders, prospective investors, or just interested observers. Appearances at a hearing in September of 1971 to consider the sale of several subsidiaries in the Chapter X proceedings of Beck Industries listed no less than twenty-one law firms.

Aside from the advantages to the regular bankruptcy practitioners—a bankruptcy attorney who files a Chapter X case for his client is really giving the case away—Chapter XI is a much better deal than Chapter X for the owners of a troubled business.

As one attorney puts it, "What can you do for a guy in Chapter X? The court slaps a trustee in and even if the trustee keeps the management, it's the trustee who calls the shots. He can kick management out on its can anytime he wants to. Besides, in Chapter XI you can preserve stockholders' equity. In Chapter X, if the company is insolvent, the stockholders are wiped out."

The point about stockholders is widely misunderstood, even by the sophisticated Wall Street securities traders. In a Chapter X reorganization, there comes a time when the court makes a decision on the solvency of the debtor. This decision is based on a realistic audit of the firm's assets and liabilities, and if the liabilities exceed the assets, the court must rule that the company is insolvent and stockholders have no equity.

From time to time I've noticed trading in stock after there has been a court ruling that the stock has no value, apparently in the hope that a successful reorganization is possible and the stock will come back. No way. Once the court has ruled the company insolvent, the stock is officially dead and the old stockholders no longer have any interest in the proceedings. Any reorganization would necessarily involve new stockholders. The reorganization proceedings of Farrington Manufacturing Company, an electronics company, provided a recent example of Wall Street's groundless hopes.

On October 18, 1971, a notice went out to stockholders, creditors and "all other parties in interest" announcing a hearing for November 16 to determine the solvency of the company. Included in the notice were the following statements:

As reflected on the Company's consolidated balance sheet at December 31, 1970, Farrington's consolidated assets then aggregated approximately $6.5 million, and its liabilities totalled approximately $33.2 million at that date. . . .

If FMC is found to be insolvent, the shareholders will be

legally precluded from participating in any plan of reorganization or distribution of assets, and will have no further interest in the reorganization proceedings.

On the basis of this notice, it should have been fairly obvious that this stock was worthless. Yet all during November 1971 the stock was traded actively, selling between a nickel and 25 cents a share. One major over-the-counter house discontinued trading Farrington in December, but as late as February 1972 the stock still was being quoted OTC at 3 cents bid, 10 cents asked—this for stock that had been officially declared worthless by a court some three months earlier.

I asked an OTC broker how come Farrington was still being traded so long after it was declared legally dead.

"On Wall Street," he said, "hope never dies." And neither does ignorance. It's apparent to me that anyone buying the stock was doing so in the hope that the firm could be successfully reorganized and without the knowledge that even if Farrington went on to become bigger than General Motors the holder of the old stock still would not get a cent for his investment.

This matter of solvency someday will have to be decided in the Penn Central bankruptcy case. At this point the question hasn't come up, and no one knows for sure whether or not the Penn Central Transportation Company, the principal operating subsidiary of Penn Central Corporation, is solvent or not, but if the subsidiary should be declared insolvent, the stock of the parent will become virtually worthless.

Railroads cannot reorganize under Chapter X or Chapter XI. They come into the bankruptcy courts under Section 77 of the Bankruptcy Act. This proceeding is substantially the same as a Chapter X reorganization except that the Interstate Commerce Commission takes an active role in the proceedings instead of the SEC.

Chapter XI is much more popular than Chapter X, and each year more than ten times as many XIs are filed as Xs. In fiscal 1971 there were 1,792 filings under Chapter XI and only 179 under X. And small wonder.

Under Chapter XI, it's possible for an insolvent company to work down its debts through an arrangement that only a bare majority of its creditors accept, have its solvency restored through this debt reduction, avoid paying taxes on the "profit" earned from forgiven debt, issue stock without the necessity of SEC registration and get out from under burdensome leases or other long-term contracts. All this can be done without giving up control of the business to a court-appointed trustee, as would occur in Chapter X.

At this point I must note that in some jurisdictions receivers are appointed by the court to supervise arrangements (and collect a fee), but in New York Chapter XI receivers are rare. In New York the debtor is permitted to remain in possession of the company assets and to operate his business, reporting periodically to the court on how things are going.

But even in areas where receivers are appointed, they do not exercise the same degree of control or participation as a Chapter X trustee. The Chapter XI receiver's function is essentially to see that assets of the business don't go down the drain while a plan is being worked out. Although he's also responsible for the operation of the business, he will usually leave that to management.

On the other hand, the Chapter X trustee becomes

executive and sometimes even operating head of the business during the period of reorganization. Attorneys who have served in the post contend that to properly execute the functions of a trustee of a large operating corporation, full time must be devoted to it, and nobody should take the job on unless he's willing to let his law practice stagnate for a couple of years. This is not to say that Chapter X trustees are always attorneys. The more enlightened judges may appoint businesssmen with experience in the field of the company being reorganized, but lawyers are the most likely appointees.

The practice of appointing receivers in Chapter XI cases is controversial, and there is much sentiment among creditors and lawyers representing creditors for its abolishment. Receiverships accomplish little more than to add to the expenses of bankruptcy administration—already too high.

The statutory rates for receivers in bankruptcy cases are 6 percent of the first $500 coming into the estate, 4 percent of the next $1,000, 2 percent of the next $8,500 and 1 percent of the balance. These are maximums except in cases in which the receiver has a going business to run. Then he can be awarded up to twice the statutory fees. Since Chapter XI cases almost always deal with operating businesses, the receiver's cut can run high. And that's just part of the cost. As soon as a receiver is appointed, he goes out and hires himself a lawyer. The fee for the attorney for the receiver is an open-ended one and depends on how much work he does and how much money he brings into the estate.

As an indication of the relative fees of a receiver and his attorney, a bankruptcy case closed out recently with

$316,000 in the estate showed the receiver's commission at $5,993 and his attorney applying for $18,000.

Credit men generally oppose the gratuitous appointment of receivers by the courts. "Something should be done about receivers being appointed in Chapter XI proceedings out of town," says one New York credit man. "There shouldn't be any receiver appointed unless the creditors ask for it. After all, once a business is insolvent, it really belongs to the creditors. It's our company, yet these judges appoint receivers, the receivers pick attorneys and accountants and the creditors don't have a damn thing to say about it."

Referee Asa Herzog thinks all receiverships should be eliminated in Chapter XI cases and most in straight bankruptcy. In a straight bankruptcy, the receiver is interim caretaker, who looks after the assets until such time as the court calls a meeting of creditors (usually thirty to forty-five days) to elect a trustee. The receiver steps out unless he manages to get himself elected trustee.

Referee Herzog points out that under the Bankruptcy Act, the court has the option to appoint a receiver or the United States Marshal to watch over the assets until a trustee can be elected. The U.S. Marshal gets no fee, so that option is ignored.

Referee Herzog allows for exceptions to the receiverless bankruptcy concept when there is the need to operate a business for a period of time to preserve assets and there is no longer any viable management. Then and only then is there any justification for a receiver, says the referee.

Incidentally, in Manhattan Federal Court, the referees are not empowered to appoint receivers. This right has been reserved by the Federal District Court judges. However, in other jurisdictions, referees do appoint receivers.

And while we're on the subject of less than vital jobs in the bankruptcy business, there's something called "distributing agent" appointed by referees in Chapter XI cases. It is the function of the distributor to sign and mail out checks to creditors once a Chapter XI plan is confirmed.

"This," says one referee, "is patronage, plain and simple," and he concedes that he gives distributorships to lawyers he is "friendly with." Although most distributorships don't pay really big money—the average fee is about $1,000—some run to $5,000 or $10,000, depending on how much is being distributed.

"It's a job that won't try anyone's intelligence," says the referee, "and a fee of around five dollars a check is very nice."

Getting back to Chapter XI vs Chapter X, the format for whacking up the fees provides an overpowering stimulus toward Chapter XI. Any attorney with so much as a passing interest in making money will opt for XI, and at the outset the choice is up to debtor's attorney. (There is a provision for involuntary Chapter X petition, but it happens so rarely it's hardly worth mentioning. In fiscal 1971 there were nineteen involuntaries out of 179 Chapter Xs filed in the country. Chapter XI proceedings are all voluntary.)

On January 10, 1972, the court confirmed the Chapter XI plan of Visual Electronics Corporation. Visual is a public company whose stock was listed on the American Stock Exchange. Levin & Weintraub, the law firm that handled the case, was paid a $25,000 retainer, and on confirmation the court awarded the firm an additional

$125,000, bringing the total to $150,000. Had L & W brought the case in under Chapter X, they would have been lucky to keep the $25,000 retainer and Visual may never have been able to consummate a plan.

Chapter XI also offers a cut-rate route for going public. If you'd like to go public without all the fuss of registration of stock with the SEC and without getting mixed up with those slick Wall Street underwriters and securities lawyers, Chapter XI offers the ideal vehicle. Not your company's Chapter XI, but the proceedings of a public company that looks as if it's about to go under.

In general, the procedure calls for the purchase of a controlling block of stock—this comes cheap in a company about to go bankrupt—the payment of a nominal sum to creditors of the acquired company and, finally, a merger.

By merging the healthy privately owned company into the near bankrupt public company, the vehicle that emerges is a public company with a tax loss that can be used to reduce taxes against future profits. The new public company will have all the privileges and advantages of a company that waded through the miles of red tape of an initial public stock issue.

Need more money? Just sell a few shares of stock. Want to buy another company? Pay off in paper. Want to keep your executives happy? Give them stock options. All this can be accomplished at bargain prices through a Chapter XI takeover.

One of my lawyer friends describes how he did it for a client:

"There was this publicly owned dress company in Chapter XI that was ready to go down the drain. There was no money for a settlement and it looked like a complete washout for creditors.

"I had a client in the same business who was doing very well and who wanted to go public. It was a small company, doing between ten and fifteen million, but I figured it still would cost us about sixty thousand to take him public with all the special lawyers' fees, audits, printing costs.

"We walked into the Chapter XI deal and bought a controlling block of stock at twenty cents a share—the stock wouldn't have been worth anything if the company had gone into bankruptcy. Then we offered the creditors a twelve percent cash settlement and they grabbed it, since they would have been skunked if there were no offer. We borrowed the money from a factor for the settlement and gave the factor a block of stock as an extra sweetener. I got some of it myself.

"When the whole thing was over, my client had got himself a public vehicle, and not only didn't it cost him anything, but he made a few bucks on it.

"Even though in a liquidation the Chapter XI company would have been a total loss for general creditors, as a going concern it was worth money. My client could use every piece of goods in the place and turn it into sales. The way I figure it, the stuff was worth about thirty-five thousand more to him than he paid out in the settlement, and that includes fees and the rest of the expenses. Take that and add it to the sixty thousand it would have cost him to go public along the traditional route, and my boy made around a hundred thousand on the deal."

Chapter XI plans can be simple settlements or complex formulas employing various classes of stock, notes, debentures or profit-sharing schemes. You give the creditors whatever circumstances dictate and they're willing to accept.

A special problem arises in a stock payout—how to evaluate stock of an insolvent corporation? By traditional accounting methods such stock is worth zero. But it must be given a value in order to pay the referee's Salary and Expense Fund. Before a plan is confirmed, provision must be made to pay the fund 3 percent of the first $100,000 of obligations paid or extended in the plan and 1½ percent of the balance. You can give your creditors the business, but the court wants cash. (The fund has been running in the red since 1966, and the idea of a self-supporting bankruptcy court system is being abandoned. Payments will continue, but they will go to the treasury instead of the special fund.)

The question of stock value is resolved through hearings and expert testimony. In the proceeding of Milo Electronics, a public company that worked out a stock deal with creditors in Chapter XI, the stock, which was trading over the counter at $3 a share, was evaluated at $1.20 a share for the purposes of the proceeding. The lower value was chosen because of the dilution factor resulting from the large number of shares to be issued under the plan.

There appears to be a cloud of doubt on whether stock obtained in payment of a Chapter XI plan can be freely traded without SEC registration. However, it is being done all the time and nobody is hollering.

As I mentioned earlier, a majority of creditors in number and amount of claims must accept a Chapter XI plan to get confirmation. But that's not all. The plan also must be found feasible and to the best interest of creditors. The test for feasibility is simply: Can the plan be implemented? If it's a cash plan and the money is available, there's no problem. The plan is obviously feasible. But if payments are to run over a period of time, there must be some showing that there's a reasonable prospect that the money will be there when the payments come due. Some referees hold long hearings with cash-flow projections and business analyses and expert witnesses to determine feasibility. Others just put the officer of the debtor company on the witness stand and ask, "Is this plan feasible?" If the answer is "yes," that covers feasibility.

For a plan to be in the "best interest of creditors" it must be shown that creditors will be getting more under the plan than they would get if the business were liquidated in bankruptcy. If creditors are being offered 20 percent under the plan and estimates indicate that selling the assets under the hammer would bring 35 percent, this plan would not be in the creditors' best interest.

Here again we're dealing with intangibles, and the fact that creditors accepted a plan is *prima facie* evidence that it's to their best interest.

But there is no way of knowing for sure. In the spring of 1961 Crawford Clothes, a major chain of men's clothing stores, ran into financial troubles and filed a Chapter XI petition. After some negotiating a 37½ percent plan was accepted by creditors and the deal was all set to go when the merchant who had come in to finance the plan backed out. He had been operating a clothing chain of his own and decided he was too old to get tangled with a headache the size of Crawford Clothes. He had posted a good-faith deposit of $100,000 to bind his deal and he just walked away, leaving the $100,000 to become part of the estate of Crawford Clothes, Inc., bankruptcy case number 61-B-438, United States District Court for the Southern District of New York.

It took ten years to close out the case, but when it was over creditors, whose claims totaled about $2.5 million, had been paid 80 percent and there was plenty left over for fees.

The trustee, New York Credit Men's Adjustment Bureau, was paid commissions of $38,349; the trustee's attorney, Hahn, Hessen, Margolis & Ryan, got a cool $326,000; the accountants for the trustee and debtor-in-possession, Wasserman & Taten, $51,000; and there was another $30,000 or so divided up among an assortment of attorneys and appraisers. The Referees' Salary and Expense Fund netted $76,448 from the case.

Referee Herzog, who administered the case, was ecstatic in his final report recommending the fees. The referee characterized as "nothing less than sheer genius" a plan devised by the trustee's counsel, setting up the former head of Crawford's collection department in business to collect the chain's receivables. He pointed out that the best offer for the receivables in bulk was $260,000 and that through this method and "another brilliant idea" (using First National City Bank branches as collection points) over $1 million was collected on the $1,400,000 due from 36,000 customers.

Crawford's was also the vehicle for a major breakthrough in bankruptcy administration. Prior to the Crawford case, all cash in bankruptcy estates was kept in noninterest-bearing demand deposits. This meant that millions of dollars were tied up for years doing nothing but making bankers very happy. The bankers loved the old system but creditors hated it.

In his final report, Referee Herzog noted that while there was nothing in the Bankruptcy Act that prohibited a trustee from putting money in interest-bearing time deposits, there was no authorization for such deposits and it was customary to keep trustees' funds in ordinary checking accounts. Demonstrating "initiative and imagination," the counsel for the Crawford trustee placed funds in time interest-bearing deposits more than a year before a law was passed specifically authorizing such deposits, "thus earning a substantial sum of money for this estate."

The Crawford case is cited as living proof that there's no truth to the charge that creditors never get anything in bankruptcy.

But figures compiled by the Administrative Office of the United States Courts* show the Crawford case was most unusual. Of the bankruptcy cases closed in 1969, there were 107,481 with no assets at all, 23,777 in which all the assets went for administrative expenses and 22,355 asset cases.

The asset cases realized a total of $113,136,826 out of which unsecured creditors got $30,810,542. The rest went for administration expenses, $26,446,037; secured creditors, $37,499,860; priority claims (taxes, wages, etc.), $14,698,592; and miscellaneous, $3,681,785.

In other words, we find more cases in which administration expenses consumed all the available assets than cases in which there was some distribution to general creditors. Furthermore, where there was distribution, less than one

* Published in the September 1971 issue of *Credit and Financial Management* magazine.

third of the money paid out went to the lowly unsecured creditor.

While the above figures pertain to bankruptcy liquidation and not Chapter XI or Chapter X proceedings, the high cost of administration is a factor in any insolvency.

For this reason out-of-court settlements, where feasible, are regarded as the least of the available evils. Settlements can be arranged quickly and neatly, and while the fees aren't as large as in court proceedings, there is infinitely less work involved.

Administration expenses in out-of-court settlements run to about 5 percent of liabilities, though this will vary from case to case. In very small cases, the fees may come to 10 percent, while in the million-dollar deals the lawyers and accountants will be happy with a smaller percentage, although the actual fee will be larger.

A recent case handled through the New York Credit Men's Adjustment Bureau settled $550,000 in debt for 20 percent cash with just a couple of meetings and a time span of ninety days from the first meeting to the payment of settlement. The debtor's lawyer got $3,500 in a retainer and another $2,500 when it was over; the creditors' committee counsel was paid $3,500; the committee accountant got $3,000; and the Bureau got $1,000. Everybody was satisfied.

In Chapter XI, the same deal would take at least six months, with much more paperwork and bigger fees.

But there are difficulties in staying out of court. If there are a great many creditors scattered all over the country, there's no way to get them to act in concert without going to court for protection against lawsuits and attachments. If just a few creditors don't like the settlement offer, they

can scuttle it. New credit can't be arranged without creditor cooperation. The smaller and tighter knit the creditor
body, the better the chances for out-of-court deals. (New
credit isn't easy to get in Chapter XI either, but at least
the court does make a provision to give new creditors an
edge over the old debt.)

Other factors may also induce a court proceeding. For
instance, both Chapter X and Chapter XI provide for
rejection of burdensome executory contracts. If a company is locked into a $100,000-a-year employment con-
tract with an executive who doesn't produce but who
won't go away either, this contract can be rejected.

The most common type of contracts subject to rejection
are long-term leases. In the 1950s and 1960s, when there
was a great surge of retailers moving to suburban shopping centers, many chains were caught with expensive,
long-term leases in deteriorating downtown shopping
areas. The stronger chains were able to phase out money-
losing downtown units and absorb the losses, while others,
including Grayson-Robinson, went into the bankruptcy
courts and rejected leases on a grand scale.

The rejection of a lease doesn't let the lessee off scot-
free, but damages are scaled down materially.

Taxes are another consideration. If a firm settles
$500,000 worth of debts for 50 cents on the dollar, the
$250,000 saved must be recorded as a profit and taxes
paid on it. Chapter XI specifically exempts this type of
profit from taxation.

And never forget fees. The attorney for a company in
Chapter XI can build up a much better case for a big fee
than he can in a quick out-of-court settlement. On the
other hand, the creditors' representatives, such as attor-

neys, accountants and secretaries, are dealing in a much friendlier atmosphere when the creditors' committee rules on fees rather than the courts. After all, the committee members put them into the case in the first place, so they're not likely to stiff them when the fees are passed out.

Just one more point about fees. If you ever want to give a bankruptcy attorney a quick case of heartburn, just say 60-d. That's the section under which attorneys are forced to give back a portion of their fee if the court or some other party interested in the proceeding thinks the payment was excessive. The lawyer who stays out of court with his settlement doesn't have to worry about being 60-d'd out of his fee.

The 60-d problem comes up most frequently when Chapter XI proceedings are aborted and become straight bankruptcies. The attorney for a debtor grabs a retainer as soon as he takes a Chapter XI on, and the fee is based on work anticipated in carrying through a successful plan. If the proceeding falls apart, the attorney may not have done enough to earn the retainer, at least not in the eyes of the trustee who takes over the administration of the case in bankruptcy. The trustee's attorney is most likely to discover that the retainer was excessive when he looks at the estate and figures there may not be enough in it to pay his own fee. So the trustee's lawyer will move under 60-d to force the debtor's attorney to give up a part of the retainer.

The amount returned can be substantial. In one recent case an attorney took a retainer of $15,000, worked about nine months to bring the case right up to the point of confirmation, but the financing fell through and the case went into bankruptcy. The trustee brought a 60-d action and the debtor's lawyer offered to settle by returning $2,500. The trustee's lawyer wanted $5,000, and there was a tentative agreement at $3,500. But that agreement collapsed; there was a full-scale trial of the issue and the referee ruled that $12,000 of the $15,000 should be returned. You wouldn't believe the language the learned member of the bar used to describe his feelings toward the referee and the trustee's lawyer.

Although there are substantive differences among Chapter XI, Chapter X and out-of-court settlements, there is a common denominator—they all spell bad news. As far as creditors are concerned, it's a matter of degree.

Aside from straight bankruptcy or assignments for the benefit of creditors, Chapter X stands at the top of the "Who needs it?" list. Whether justified or not, Chapter X has a bad image and is equated in the minds of credit men with endless hearings, fees of monumental proportions, ultimate liquidation and zero recoveries. When a company goes into Chapter X reorganization, the average creditor shrugs his shoulders and figures it's all so complicated, he may just as well forget the whole thing.

When a Chapter XI petition for an arrangement is filed, the creditor figures he's going to take a beating but at least he has a better idea of what's happening and is able to follow and even take an active part in the proceedings.

The out-of-court settlement is simplest and, from the creditor's point of view, the most controllable. Of the various alternatives, this is what he dislikes the least.

9 Even Millionaires Go Broke

Most individual bankruptcies arise from shopping sprees at Bloomingdale's or similar abuses of easy credit. Excesses are found on both sides of the credit coin—credit-card people pushing the joys of living beyond one's means and the consumer responding with an overabundance of enthusiasm. These cases work their way through the bankruptcy courts with hardly a ripple, and nobody except those directly involved pays any attention. But every once in a while comes a case that raises eyebrows clear across the country.

Such was the Chapter XI proceeding of Lammot du Pont Copeland, Jr., the scion of one of America's wealthiest families. It seemed inconceivable that the family would permit the du Pont name to be dragged through the bankruptcy courts just for a lousy $55 million or so, but dragged through the courts it was. The du Pont label also took something of a kicking around in the New York brokerage community, a story I'll discuss later in this volume.

Mr. Copeland got himself into a hopeless financial bind

through an orgy of business ventures that ranged from motion-picture distribution to land speculation to cattle feeding to shopping-center construction to trucking and warehousing to newspaper publishing to toy manufacturing.

In his mid-thirties at the time of the bankruptcy, Mr. Copeland blamed his troubles on a mysterious financier, mortgage broker and real-estate speculator named Thomas A. Shaheen, who midway in the proceedings disappeared with three separate contempt-of-court charges hanging over him. Mr. Shaheen failed to appear in court in a fraud case in Chicago and had two contempt citations in the Copeland proceedings. One was for nonappearance and the other for failure to answer certain questions. Mr. Shaheen had been subjected to lengthy questioning in the bankruptcy courts before ducking out.

Mr. Copeland had complete faith in Mr. Shaheen, and when attorneys were trying to convince the du Pont heir that his finances were in such a tangle that the bankruptcy courts offered the only way out, he stalled for weeks telling them that Mr. Shaheen would somehow bring help and solve all the financial problems.

A banker who had some touchy dealings with Mr. Copeland described him as a "nice-looking Ivy League type, soft-spoken . . . a likable, decent sort of fellow, but not smart. Based on his business judgments about some of the things he got into, he'd have had to be deaf, dumb and blind to go after some of those deals. He just was not smart about business matters. I don't think he ever figured out what business was all about."

The Copeland case threw the sleepy little bankruptcy office in Wilmington into a turmoil. The office was not set up for multimillion-dollar bankruptcies or the great hordes of lawyers that would be swarming in from around the county. At the first meeting of creditors that stretched over two days in November 1970, some fifty attorneys representing the cream of the American legal profession put in an appearance.

Wilmington didn't even have a full-time referee. It was one of the few remaining districts in which the volume of cases was too small to justify full-time bankruptcy administration.

The bankruptcy court was presided over by Murray Schwartz, a forty-year-old attorney whose basic income came from his private law practice. A partner in the Wilmington law firm of Longobardi & Schwartz, the part-time referee was appointed to the bench in August of 1969. A little over a year later Referee Schwartz was hit with what he called "this administrative horror"—the Copeland case. By December of 1971 the transcripts of testimony, documentary evidence, orders, applications, motions, briefs—all the legal paraphernalia that befuddle the layman and make the lawyers rich—had already filled three filing-cabinet drawers. Just one of those drawers could accommodate the files of fifty or more ordinary bankruptcy cases.

A year after the proceeding started, Richards, Layton & Finger, the Wilmington law firm that represented Mr. Copeland, had logged over 5,000 man hours of working time on the case. On the basis of a forty-hour work week, that comes to about two and a half years. And the proceeding was a long way from a conclusion.

(Charles Seligson, an expert in bankruptcy law, was called in from New York to serve with the Wilmington firm as special counsel for dealing with the major moves in the case.)

Most of Mr. Copeland's debts stemmed from personal guarantees in this weird assortment of ventures—a large number of which were channeled through the Winthrop Lawrence Corporation, a holding company headed by Mr. Shaheen. Mr. Copeland owned a 37½ percent interest in Winthrop Lawrence.

Much of the action took place in the 1968–69 period when mergers were not only fashionable but a national sickness. It was a period when easy money was being made by taking two corporate dogs and putting them together with two other corporate dogs, and instead of getting four the masters of synergism were getting five— and selling them at sixty times earnings.

A look through the massive court records in the Copeland case gave the impression that the young du Pont heir was trying to corner the market in kooky speculations.

His method was to use the magic du Pont name to cosign to guarantee or to participate, and what bank would say no to such a guarantor. They said yes in big numbers and many were sorry.

The list of banks with claims against Copeland read like the roster for a national convention of the American Bankers Association. Just about every section of the country was represented.

In the far West there were the North Denver Bank in Denver and the Peoples Bank in Aurora, Colorado. The Southwest was covered by the Republic National Bank of Dallas and the Houston Bank & Trust Company, Houston.

In the Midwest, we had the Missouri State Bank & Trust Company, St. Louis; the University National Bank

in Chicago; First National Bank of Carrollton, Sherrods-
ville, Ohio; and the Huntington National Bank, Colum-
bus, Ohio.

In the deep South there were the Hancock Bank,
Gulfport, Mississippi, and the First National Bank of
Mobile. The East was represented by the First National
Bank of Lafayette, Chevy Chase, Maryland; the Wilming-
ton Trust Company, Wilmington; and Royal National
Bank of New York, among others. Lending an interna-
tional flavor were the Union Bank of Switzerland and
Banco Crédito y Ahorro Ponceño of Puerto Nuevo, Puerto
Rico.

And this is just a partial list. There were more banks,
union pension funds and an assortment of other creditors.

A personal financial statement showing a net worth of
$20,299,000 as of April 30, 1970, was described as "defec-
tive" by Copeland in his testimony before Referee
Schwartz. He said the figures overstated the net worth of
Winthrop Lawrence at $4.4 million and failed to include
all of his contingent debts. The du Pont heir testified that
he withdrew the statement, but conceded that some
copies did get around.

One section of the April 30 financial statement that was
particularly interesting had to do with Copeland's trust
funds. Not too many people go into bankruptcy court
with trust-fund interests worth $9.3 million, and in this
case his creditors couldn't touch a penny of the principal
or interest. The fact that the value of the funds was included in the statement and comprised about half of
Copeland's stated net worth didn't make any difference.

The trusts were set up as so-called "spendthrift trusts,"
and Copeland's attorneys maintained that under Dela-

ware law that money is out of reach of creditors.

Copeland's income from the trusts was not inconsiderable. In 1968 they brought him $299,668, and in 1969 the income was $311,697.

Copeland also managed to retain his home, a $554,461 hunk of real estate at fashionable West of Rising Sun Lane, Christiana Hundred, Delaware. The property was covered by a lien obtained by the Wilmington Trust Company, a bank that, if not controlled by the du Pont family, was certainly under its influence. For one thing, the bank was trustee for millions in du Pont family trusts.

The transaction was highly complex, as was just about everything about the case, but pieced together from the court records, the house was kept in the family and out of the reach of other creditors like this:

Copeland had a loan outstanding from the Wilmington Trust Company of $3,461,332 which was secured by the real estate and some $300,000 worth of marketable securities. The loan was also guaranteed by Lammot du Pont Copeland, Sr. Precisely four months and one day before the younger Copeland filed his Chapter XI petition, the Wilmington Trust entered a judgment against him and took over the collateral.

The timing was crucial. Under the Bankruptcy Act, transactions that occur within four months of the filing of a petition can be attacked and set aside. In other words, the judgment the Wilmington bank obtained might have been nullified if the petition had been filed sooner.

Lammot du Pont Copeland, Jr., filed his Chapter XI petition on October 20, 1970. The petition maintained that the debtor was unable to pay his debts as they matured and that he intended to propose a plan of arrangement for paying off creditors.

Referee Schwartz issued the customary restraining order to block creditors from grabbing assets and to maintain the status quo while the lawyers tried to unsnarl the complicated financial muddle and come up with a workable plan.

Originally, the petition listed total debts of $62,872,298. A month later the figures were amended, reducing the liabilities to $55,371,343. Assets were shown as $24,055,-912 and excluded the trust funds, which were claimed as exempt.

However, an analysis of the assets showed that they were closer to zero than to $24 million. Every major asset either was hocked to secure loans or guarantees or was of dubious value because it represented an investment in a busted company.

Liabilities diminish as collateral is liquidated, but they rarely dissolve as quickly as assets. In the bankruptcy business, assets are rarely worth what they're listed at, but the liabilities are as good as gold.

The biggest part of Copeland's debt was made up of "accommodation paper." He had the fastest pen in the East and became one of history's most accommodating men. He ran up nearly $33 million in accommodation paper, mainly by signing guarantees for companies in which he had an interest.

A good part of the accommodation was for the benefit of Winthrop Lawrence Corporation, the free-wheeling holding company.

These accommodations included:

A $2,525,000 note to Distrifilm, S.A. for the distribution rights in the United States and Canada to five films produced by London Screenplay, Ltd., of London.

A $6.5 million loan from the Union Bank of Switzerland

which was guaranteed by Copeland and collateralized by a variety of securities, including about $3.8 million worth of Copeland's father's assets. The debt to UBS was knocked down to $2.1 million through liquidation of the collateral.

A guarantee to purchase 50,000 shares of Transogram Company, Inc., at $8 a share, exposing him to a $400,000 liability.

A guarantee of $3.8 million for the purchase of 750,000 shares of Transogram stock.

An agreement to repurchase 30,000 shares of Transogram at $20 a share, setting up a liability of $600,000.

There were so many guarantees floating around that Copeland forgot to list in his court papers the guarantee of a $250,000 note of the Gulf Coast Institute, a 95 percent-owned subsidiary of Winthrop Lawrence. The note was used to acquire the lease of a hotel in Raleigh, North Carolina.

Copeland told of this oversight during his testimony before the referee. He said he also omitted by inadvertence a $237,500 asset item representing oil leases. He added, however, that the oil investment was all tied up in litigation.

Winthrop Lawrence entered a claim for $2,721,659 against Copeland which he disputed. The court papers said the Winthrop Lawrence claim was for "alleged payments made on behalf of debtor" during 1967–70.

On top of all the accommodations, Copeland listed secured claims of $13,444,174. The value of the collateral pledged to secure the debts totaled only $12.2 million, so there was a deficit in this category.

General unsecured creditors listed came to $8,808,206

and ranged from the $4.2 million debt to the Republic National Bank of Dallas to $33 owing to the Burlingame Country Club of Hillsborough, California, for unpaid dues.

He testified that he borrowed the $4.2 million from Republic National to relend it to Campus Centers, Inc. In return for the loan he got a $100,000 fee and a $4.2 million second mortgage on a dormitory located on the campus of Southwest Louisiana State University in Lafayette, Louisiana.

This was typical of the kind of deal Copeland got himself involved in.

Listen to his explanation of another, taken from the 347-page transcript of his testimony at the first meeting of creditors in November 1970:

Question by Referee Schwartz:

The next item, Super Stores, Inc., can you explain how you are a guarantor on that?

A: Yes. I individually owned a shopping center in Sacramento, California, which I first transferred to Winthrop Lawrence for preferred stock in Winthrop Lawrence, and then Winthrop Lawrence in turn transferred it to Super Stores, Inc., for 500,000 shares of the Common Stock of Super Stores, which represented about 60 [percent] ownership in that company.

This shopping center was leased by Super Stores to an entity which I owned, called Liberty Land, Inc., which in turn sublet the store to Rosko Stores, which is a part of Gamble-Skogmo, Inc., who were operating the store.

As part of this I guaranteed the payment of the lease to Super Stores by Liberty Land.

Q: Do you still own all of Liberty Land?

A: Yes.

The result of all this paper churning, according to Copeland's testimony, was that he would be on the hook for a $50,000 to $60,000 deficit on the lease for the then current fiscal year.

Another typically complex financing operation described by Copeland involved Verdugo Hills, 785 acres of raw land around Burbank, California.

He testified that he put $1 million of his own money into Verdugo Hills but got it out through a second mortgage on the land. Then he acquired 120,000 shares of Canaveral International Corporation, a land-development and mobile-home company, which he transferred in November 1969 to Transogram, his toy-making venture, for 60,000 shares of Transogram stock. This, he said, was part of the deal under which Winthrop Lawrence took control of Transogram.

So if we eliminate all the complications, we find that Copeland paid $1 million for Transogram stock that was practically worthless at the time of his insolvency.

Copeland told of another real-estate deal with a subsidiary of Canaveral International in which he bought a tract of land in Freeport in the Bahamas. He paid $800,000 for the land, and Freeport Ridge, the Canaveral subsidiary, was supposed to sell it in small parcels over three years and pay Copeland $900,000.

Sounds like a simple transaction, but nothing was simple in the Copeland case. After buying the Freeport property, he gave Winthrop Lawrence a $750,000 mortgage on it, which Winthrop Lawrence assigned to a company called United International for a block of unregistered stock representing a 35 percent interest in United.

United International then pledged the mortgage to

Madison National Bank for a $450,000 loan.

Copeland's propensity for guaranteeing things got him into Dean Van Lines, a California trucking company. In early 1968 he guaranteed a $1.6 million loan for Dean and received an option to buy 25 percent of the stock for $500,000.

Dean soon needed more help, and Copeland picked up his option with a note for $500,000. Things apparently worsened, and Dean went into a Chapter XI proceeding in October of 1968. Copeland and his companies helped to finance Dean during the trucking firm's Chapter XI, and when a plan was put through, the Copeland interests wound up with about 800,000 of the 1.1 million Dean Van shares outstanding.

With another stroke of his pen Copeland acquired a 31 percent interest in a California cattle-feeding ranch. His cost: the guarantee of a $1.5 million mortgage on the property held by the Connecticut Mutual Life Insurance Company.

Getting back to the status of the formidable-looking list of assets set forth in the Copeland petition, there was included some $3.9 million worth of marketable securities. Now marketable securities are usually as good as money in the bank.

But checking through a prodigious set of footnotes disclosed that out of the $3.9 million, only about $29,000 of the securities were not in hock.

Free and clear were such items as $1,897 in Decatur Income Fund, $2,024 in the Delaware Fund and $644 in Delta Trend Fund. He was, incidentally, a director of all three funds.

Outside of the marketable securities, Copeland listed

$12 million worth of investments in such gilt-edged companies as Winthrop Lawrence, Transogram and Standard Media, all three of which were in Chapter XI proceedings; Graphic Productions, which was in straight bankruptcy; and Dean Van Lines, which was alive but shaking.

His real estate, shown at a cost of $7.7 million, was completely encumbered.

The house at West of Rising Sun Lane was covered by a lien of the Wilmington Trust. He also owned a group of residential houses in Wilmington that he rented out. These too were under the Wilmington Trust umbrella.

Then there was the Verdugo Hills property. This was listed at a cost of $1,567,304, subject to mortgages totaling $1.6 million.

The real estate included a Holiday Inn motel and shopping arcade in Chevy Chase, Maryland, listed at $6.6 million and subject to mortgages of the same amount.

There was a two-story commercial building in Phoenix, Arizona, with a listed value of $303,921 and a mortgage of $547,842.

And finally there was a tract of undeveloped land near Houston, Texas—Red Bluff Townhouses—which cost a half million and was covered by a mortgage for that amount.

By the end of 1971 the Chevy Chase property, the Phoenix real estate and the land near Houston had been sold off and all three deals resulted in a wash. The proceeds just covered the encumbrances.

Thus little could be expected for creditors from the real estate.

About the only area where some real money could be

found was in the trust funds, but the du Pont family lawyers had done a good job of protecting that money.

The personal financial statement of Copeland dated April 30, 1970, had a fairly detailed description of the trusts.

One group, from which he was receiving a lifetime income, had a market value of something over $2.3 million. But, the accountants stated, "Using the U.S. Treasury Department tables to calculate the value of Mr. Copeland's Life Estates results in a computed valuation of $3,600,300."

His remainder interest in these trusts was calculated at $1,998,667.

His prospective interest in another group of trusts worth $69 million was calculated at $3,229,150. He comes into one third of the income on these trusts upon the death of the present life income beneficiary.

His interest in a third group of trusts was computed to be worth $485,674. This group had a market value "in excess of $2.4 million," and Copeland came in as a one-third lifetime beneficiary on December 27, 1970.

In addition to these trusts, the financial statement pointed out that the income from another $8 million was going to charity, but over the following fifteen years one third of that income would flow to Copeland. The value of this interest and of interests in other trusts was not included in the $9.3 million valuation of Copeland's trust fortune, according to the statement.

The schedules of assets and liabilities filed by Copeland in the Chapter XI proceeding listed some eighty-three trusts but fixed no value on them since they were claimed as exempt.

Summing up the assets in the Copeland Chapter XI estate: There were real estate mortgaged to the hilt, marketable investments with only $28,997 unpledged and about $12 million invested in companies that were either broke or near broke. The schedules set forth another $100,000 or so of miscellaneous assets, but unpaid United States taxes of $229,459 which must be paid in full more than covered those items.

On the liability side, the secured claims of about $13.5 million were pretty much washed out through liquidation of the collateral, leaving unsecured claims of $8.8 million and the $33 million in accommodation paper.

Assuming those debts could be whittled down to a total $20 million, the case still looked like a good deal at 10 cents on the dollar.

Despite all the wheeling and dealing that obviously occurred before Copeland came into the bankruptcy courts, there was no independent accountant retained to verify and investigate the many financial facets of the case.

The problem was money. The creditors' committee applied to the court for appointment of an accountant to conduct a preliminary investigation. The auditor's fee would have been a maximum of $25,000. But the referee turned the application down, holding that there was no provision in the law authorizing an accountant for the creditors to be paid by the debtor's estate. As for the creditors themselves, they apparently had taken enough of a bath and were not about to spend any more of their money for an investigation.

10 Bankruptcy—Wall Street Style

When Ira Haupt & Company, a major brokerage firm, collapsed in 1963, it nearly carried the rest of Wall Street down with it. The failure came within a few days of President John F. Kennedy's assassination, and the nation's nerves had been rubbed raw.

Ira Haupt's customers were literally banging on the doors of the company's locked offices, and only quick action by other brokers effectively headed off what could have been an old-fashioned run-on-the-bank panic. The Wall Street community banded together and raised a special fund to pay off Haupt's public customers. Without the fund, customers who had securities or cash on deposit with Haupt would have been in no better legal position to collect their money than the telephone company or someone who had sold Haupt paper clips.

But since public confidence was at stake, self-preservation motivated the financial community to act. Haupt's offices had closed on November 20, 1963, and on November 22 President Kennedy was shot.

Since then there has been a special arrangement for

handling insolvent brokers. And during the great blood-bath of 1969–70, when hundreds of brokers went out of business, the Special Trust Fund became a source of funds not only for public stockholders but for bankruptcy practitioners and attorneys with expertise in securities, anti-trust and other fields.

The Haupt case was handled by Charles Seligson and his associate, Harvey R. Miller. The experience and exposure gained in Haupt led to their involvement (as attorneys) in some sixteen other brokerage liquidations growing out of the paperwork jam of 1968 and the bear market of 1969–70.

Some of the firms were liquidated through bankruptcy proceedings, but, where possible, liquidations were kept out of court. There is no question that bankruptcy inflates liquidation costs.

Going back to Ira Haupt, that failure differed from the run of 1969–70 broker shutdowns. There was no Wall Street crisis filling the headlines in 1963. The failure came out of nowhere. Haupt was a victim of the salad-oil swindle in which warehouse receipts were issued for non-existent soybean oil, and huge trades were being made in commodities that weren't there. The swindle put Haupt out of business and forced the warehousing subsidiary of the mighty American Express Company to file under Chapter XI to work out a compromise with the ware-housing firm's creditors.

Liquidations of brokerage firms under the best of cir-cumstances are messy affairs. There are so many things going on at the same time, securities moving around, trades being made, shares in hock, shares out of hock, screwed-up records. It's impossible to get the business to stand still so you can see where you're at.

On top of the normal complexities, confusion at Haupt was compounded by loose ends arising from the original fraud. As for the fees involved in this kind of case, they should be enough to send every red-blooded greedy American boy racing off to law school.

There were about $38 million worth of claims filed in the Haupt proceedings, and eight years after the case came to the bankruptcy court there were still years of legal work ahead.

Through the end of 1971, Seligson & Morris, attorneys for the trustee, had been paid three-quarters of a million dollars. Charles Seligson, the trustee, waived any participation in the law firm's fee, but should collect about $100,000 in commissions. (Seligson & Morris was dissolved during the proceedings, with Messrs. Seligson and Miller moving over to Weil, Gotshal & Manges.)

A half-million-dollar fee has been paid to special counsel in a suit against American Express which was settled for $2.5 million. Another suit, this against Fidelty and Casualty Insurance Company, was settled for $6 million in June of 1972, and the attorneys handling that action were awarded $150,000 for their efforts. The accountants for the trustee were paid $350,000. Before the case is closed, there will be lots more.

Because of the injection of $9.5 million by the New York Stock Exchange trust fund, Haupt creditors came out pretty well.

Customer accounts were cleaned up quickly before the case ever got to court. Haupt had 22,000 such accounts, and in about four months all but 600 were paid off. The 600 special situations involved disputed accounts, record discrepancies and the like, and it took about three and a half years in the bankruptcy proceedings to clear them up.

On March 24, 1964, four months after Haupt went broke, three limited partners forced the company into bankruptcy. They were trying to get back some of their investment and, by pressing their claim, got themselves a $1.6 million settlement.

Ordinarily, investors in bankrupt companies are in worse shape than general creditors, but things are different on Wall Street.

In the brokerage business, capital investments can be either in cash or securities. However, if securities are used, they must be given a "haircut." This haircut has varied, but at the time of the Haupt investment $100,000 worth of stock would be taken in as $70,000 in figuring capital.

The limited partners had put in stock and claimed that the portion of their investment that represented the haircut should be treated on a par with public customer accounts.

In other words, they argued that $30,000 out of each $100,000 they put in was really a credit balance that should be paid in full along with other customer credit balances. The banks, which were the principal creditors of Haupt, disagreed and contended that the limited partners' claims should be way down on the bottom of the pile. The banks wanted the limited partners to wait until everyone else was paid in full before any participation. After seven years of bitter litigation, the partners won the $1.6 million settlement, representing about 95 percent of their "haircut" and 7½ percent of the balance of their claims.

As of this writing, the banks and the New York Stock

Exchange remain the only unpaid creditors. At the time of the failure, a group of ten banks were into Haupt for about $34.5 million. When the NYSE moved in to set up the plan for paying off the public customers, the banks made their own contribution. A formula was worked out under which the banks deferred $2 of debt for each $1 the Stock Exchange put up. With this arrangement, the banks were paid $15.5 million before the bankruptcy and were left with unpaid claims totaling $19 million. The NYSE has entered a claim for $9.5 million and will share in any final distribution. About $6 million in miscellaneous creditors have been paid in full.

Just how much the NYSE will recover or how much the banks will get is still unknown. In September of 1972 the estate had about $10 million in the till and a raft of litigation still pending. Among the live cases were: a $36 million anti-trust suit against a major produce exchange and a $4.8 million suit against an international vegetable-oil dealer the trustee claims should have known about the empty storage tanks.

So there's still plenty of room for the legal fees to pile up.

The background for the rash of liquidations that hit the brokerage business, starting in 1968, is something of a paradox. Only on Wall Street do you go broke because business is so good. Trading volume was high, stock prices were going up and a feeling of euphoria pervaded the entire industry. There was no place to go but up.

Brokers expanded their staffs—particularly in sales—let expenses fly and bought a lot of fancy equipment that some companies never even learned to work. The big problem in those beautiful days of 1967–68 was the back-office backlog. Money kept pouring in, and if there were a few billion in undelivered securities, there was no time to worry about it.

The wheels were turning, the players were putting down their bets and stock prices kept shooting ahead.

In December of 1968, as the stock market poised to begin an eighteen-month skid, the value of undelivered securities reached a peak of $4,127,000,000. To put this figure in perspective, I might note the combined net worth of Merrill Lynch, Pierce, Fenner & Smith and Bache & Company, the number-one and number-two firms in the business, comes to less than $500 million.

When the market went sour, it wasn't just a matter of stock prices going down. Volume dried up and brokers found themselves with investments in securities that were falling through the floor while the flood of commission money slowed to a trickle. Besides, the back-office problems left over from the boom years wouldn't go away.

Two of the most horrendous examples of brokerage firms with complete operations breakdowns were Goodbody & Company and F. I. du Pont, Glore, Forgan & Company. As in the Haupt case, the financial community felt that public confidence was at stake, so a major effort was made to keep the two companies afloat.

In November of 1970 an emergency marriage was arranged between Goodbody and Merrill Lynch, one of the few firms considered strong enough financially and operationally to take on the monumental headache of unscrambling the mess at Goodbody. The NYSE report on the deal points out that eighteen firms were approached and seventeen declined.

"As a last resort, Merrill Lynch agreed to take this on, and reluctantly."

In order to persuade Merrill Lynch to go along, the
exchange members committed $20 million to cover any
losses Merrill Lynch might suffer from the takeover and
another $10 million to indemnify Merrill Lynch for pos-
sible damages that could arise from an assortment of
lawsuits pending against Goodbody.

By July of the following year, the Goodbody deficit was
estimated at $24.3 million, so the entire $20 million was
needed, and Merrill Lynch was left to eat another $4.3
million. This deficit, an NYSE report said, arose from
reserves "provided for estimated losses which may arise
with respect to unresolved security differences, unconfirmed securities held by transfer agents, customer accounts in deficit, and unconfirmed debit balances in
dividend and suspense accounts." Merrill Lynch's actual
loss on the Goodbody takeover came to $6.2 million,
written off in 1971, and another $2 million in the first half
of 1972.

Total discrepancies at Goodbody came to $75 million.
This wiped out the firm's capital and left a huge deficit.
Although Goodbody was not liquidated in the formal
sense, the Merrill Lynch marriage resulted in a sharp
cutback of the Goodbody operation. Of the ninety-nine
Goodbody offices operating when Merrill Lynch moved
in, only thirty-two were left just one year later. Of Goodbody's 3,200 employees, about 2,000 were still with Merrill
Lynch a year after the merger.

If this $75 million sounds like a lot of money to dis-
appear from sloppy bookkeeping, consider F. I. du Pont,
Glore, Forgan & Company. In this case securities discrepancies came to a staggering $86 million.

When a group of investors headed by H. Ross Perot, a

Texas millionaire, decided to step into the du Pont scene in May of 1971, they put up $20 million. They received a commitment from the trust fund of another $15 million, but that would be put up only after the Perot group invested a total of $40 million.

By August, some $42 million had to be written off and another $35 million invested by Perot and his people, bringing their total investment to $55 million. Before the refinancing was completed, $79 million had been pumped into the firm.

The $42 million write-off covered part of the missing $86 million. It was hoped that the rest could be recovered through a massive follow-through effort. In September Perot told a financial writers' meeting that he had put a staff of 300 working full time, tracking down and trying to collect open items—most of which dated from 1968 through 1970.

If Wall Street didn't know what a mess du Pont was in, at least the Securities and Exchange Commission was on top of the situation. Six months after the du Pont partnership had been reorganized into a corporation and taken over by the Perot group, the SEC issued an order suspending the partnership from doing business as a broker dealer for a twelve-month period. The order was issued on November 22, 1971, and, in a masterpiece of understatement, noted that du Pont was charged with violation of securities laws by "failing accurately to make and keep current certain of its books and records."

The SEC order was academic since it applied only to the old partnership, which had ceased doing business when the Perot group stepped in.

With the astronomical sums needed to support failing brokers, it was obvious that the special trust fund, set up originally to supply $9.5 million for Haupt, was fearfully inadequate.

In December of 1970 Congress formed the Securities Investors Protection Corporation (SIPC), which could tap the United States Treasury for up to $1 billion to protect customers' cash and securities on deposit with brokers. SIPC coverage is limited to $50,000 per account with a $20,000 limit on the cash portion. There was no limit under the old special trust fund.

Meanwhile, the old trust fund still was responsible for the pre-SIPC liquidations. In July of 1971 the fund had committed $74.1 million in the liquidation of twelve NYSE member firms and the $10 million bail-out of Hayden, Stone Inc. Another $15 million was committed for du Pont, so the fund was bumping against its $90 million ceiling.

Principally because Blair & Company was forced into bankruptcy proceedings, the Exchange members had to raise the ceiling to $110 million.

As of July 1971 Blair had required $15 million from the fund for getting Blair's customers paid out. But it was expected that another $11 million would be needed to clean the case up.

In requesting the higher ceiling on July 22, the NYSE told its members:

The costs of the Blair liquidation have ballooned as a result of involuntary bankruptcy proceedings which were instituted by three subordinated investors of that firm four days after the Exchange appointed a Liquidator for the firm on September 25, 1970. Bankruptcy proceedings have substantially increased the costs incurred in the implementation of the customer assistance program. . . .

Since the onset of the bankruptcy proceeding concerning

Blair & Co., Inc., all action by the Liquidator with respect to customer accounts and property of the firm is subject to orders of the Bankruptcy Court. Protracted legal proceedings have resulted from the bankruptcy petition which continue to the present time. In April, Blair was adjudged bankrupt and in order to continue the customer assistance program, the firm was persuaded to institute proceedings under Chapter XI of the Bankruptcy Act. The success of a Chapter XI proceeding is dependent upon continued financial support by the Special Trust Fund and requires that provision be made to pay general creditors a portion of their claims on an agreed basis.

The "protracted legal proceedings" referred to by the Exchange revolve around an industrial psychologist and management consultant, Dr. John P. Foley, Jr., who put some $3 million worth of securities into Blair less than six months before the brokerage firm went broke. Dr. Foley's wife and his secretary were also in on the deal, but he was the principal investor.

The Foley group waged a bitter battle in an effort to get their money out. After losing in state court and in arbitration proceedings, the group filed an involuntary bankruptcy petition against Blair.

At the time of the investment, Blair was in violation of the net capital requirements of the Exchange and had been losing money consistently. However, Dr. Foley testified that he was told the company would move into the black by May of 1970 (he invested in Blair in April).

Blair continued to lose money and within a few months needed cash and wanted to sell out the Foley securities. Foley went to court to try to block the sale, but lost. The stock was sold and the Foley group was left with a subordinated claim. Foley then brought the involuntary bankruptcy petition against Blair, which had the effect of forcing the Blair liquidation into the courts and making life very difficult for Blair and for the Exchange. Foley's group also brought a lawsuit against Blair's officers, charging violation of securities laws.

According to a transcript of testimony in the Blair bankruptcy proceedings, Dr. Foley said that before he invested in Blair, he had also looked into the possibility of putting money into Hayden Stone, another disaster of the period. Nothing came of those talks, but to his deep regret the Blair deal was consummated.

Foley, on several occasions, testified that he took a "rooking" in the Blair case. Thus it was natural to expect that he would fight to try to salvage something from the $3 million investment.

His attorney in the bankruptcy proceeding was Leo H. Raines, an old bankruptcy campaigner who knows every wrinkle in the business and who managed to keep three referees and several U.S. district judges busy handling the mass of motions, cross-motions and appeals in the case. Blair's Chapter XI petition was filed by Mudge, Rose, Guthrie & Alexander, the law firm that once served as home base for the attaché case of President Nixon. However, most of the in-fighting was handled by Weil, Gotshal & Manges, representing the New York Stock Exchange's liquidator.

Under the Chapter XI plan offered by Blair, the Foley subordinated claim isn't worth a nickel. The plan offered Blair customers full payment but only 25 percent to other creditors. Since a subordinated claim has no value until all other creditors get full payment, the $3 million investment would be wiped out.

The Wall Street practice of financing brokerage firms with subordinated money is treacherous indeed and hopefully is being phased out. When business is good, the system works fine and a subordinated investment is an almost irresistible attraction. All you have to do is leave your stock with the broker, sign a paper and you start getting 3 percent on top of whatever your stocks already are bringing you. Your securities might be sitting with the broker anyhow, so why not take the extra income? -

But when trouble comes, subordinated capital has a way of dissolving as insiders withdraw their money. This compounds the problems, pushing the troubled firm ever closer to oblivion. At the same time, the less agile of the subordinated investors—those who don't know enough to get out or who are locked in contractually—can take a terrible drubbing.

In all, there were about $20 million in subordinated investors' claims in the Blair case. But there could have been more. Within a year prior to the bankruptcy, something over $6 million in loans were repaid, mainly to insiders.

In the statement of affairs filed in the bankruptcy proceedings, there's a list of twenty-three separate repayments ranging from $1.3 million to a senior vice-president to $12,282 to a former employee. There was a particularly heavy volume of repayments on May 29, 1970, just three days after the low point of the 1969–70 bear market. On that day alone, $3,395,954 was repaid, all to officers of the company except for $50,000 paid to the wife of an officer.

As bankruptcies go, Blair was a big one. The company showed debts of $218 million and assets of $142 million. It had 29,000 customer accounts to whom it owed about

$115 million. It was holding between $75 million and $100 million in securities owned by customers.

The "ballooning" of costs that forced the NYSE to seek another $11 million from the special trust fund came largely from the difficulties of operating in bankruptcy proceedings.

As one attorney close to the case explained, "We just couldn't make a move without getting court permission first. We were running overhead expenses of a half million dollars a month and we didn't have the flexibility in bankruptcy to cut it down quickly. There were $10 million in bank loans secured by $40 million worth of customers' securities. We had to keep on paying 8½ percent interest on those loans or the banks would foreclose and sell out the customers' stock. We had to get the court's permission to set up a control system for securities going in and out of the office.

"Because of the bankruptcy, we couldn't deliver customers' securities and we were locked into the overhead."

Finally, the overhead was brought under control and by September of 1971, about a year after the bankruptcy petition was filed, it was down to $79,000 a month. Out of the 29,000 accounts, only 4,500 were left to be worked out. The bank loans were paid off and the collateral released.

At this writing, the Foley dispute remains unresolved.

Another brokerage insolvency, in which bankruptcy proceedings have added to liquidation costs, is the Robinson & Company case in Philadelphia.

The New York Stock Exchange had sought to disown Robinson by suspending it from membership and then claiming that since Robinson was not a member, the

Exchange was not responsible for Robinson's customers. Under threats of lawsuits and other pressure, the Exchange relented and agreed to help pay out Robinson's 5,000 customers with the special fund.

Although Robinson filed its Chapter XI petition on September 1, 1970, it floundered around until January of 1971, when the NYSE came in to help.

On paper, Robinson looked virtually solvent. It showed assets of $21.6 million, including $18 million in securities at market value. Its deficiency—aside from subordinated debts—was less than a half million dollars. Yet it cost the NYSE over $1.5 million to clean up the customers' accounts.

Fees alone came to $288,000, and there is still $269,000 that may have to be paid to the Referees' Salary and Expense Fund, although the Exchange is disputing the amount.

As is the custom in Chapter XI cases in Philadelphia, a receiver was appointed. He retained two sets of attorneys, one a bankruptcy specialist and the other for the securities aspects.

The receiver was paid $147,000 for less than a year's work. In approving the commission, Referee Thomas J. Curtin pointed out that under the statute the receiver could have been paid as much as $211,637. The receiver's accountants were paid $35,000, and this was apparently another bargain since they filed an affidavit noting that they had actually spent $41,609.48. The referee was sympathetic but pointed out that since the accountants were operating under an order that limited their fee to $35,000, the fact that the job cost more than that was "just too bad."

But a battle developed over the fees for the receiver's attorneys. The bankruptcy firm had applied for $56,000 and the securities specialists asked $50,000. The New York Stock Exchange was outraged and formally objected to the applications. Harvey R. Miller, representing the Exchange, went to Philadelphia and at a long hearing before Referee Curtin on May 28, 1971, fought to get the fees cut. Miller's opposition was essentially to the fee of the securities attorneys. He told the referee he felt the bankruptcy firm's $56,000 request was fair but that based on his appraisal of the services rendered by the other firm, its fee should be cut to $29,000.

Mr. Miller brought out at the hearing that the $50,000 fee for the securities specialists broke down to an hourly billing rate of about $110. Yet more than half of the time billed by the law firm was logged by an associate whose rate was between $35 and $52 an hour. The referee apparently was impressed by Mr. Miller's arguments, and he cut the combined fee for the receiver's lawyers to $91,000 from the $106,000 requested.

11 How to Spot a Bust

It's traditional for books on financial subjects to include tips on how to get rich. Since I find it difficult to recommend bankruptcy as the road to riches, I will instead try to help you spot the other fellow's bankruptcy before it comes. While this won't get you rich, at least it may help prevent you from becoming poor. You might even pick up a couple of bucks on short sales.

First a caveat: Signals pointing out an incipient bankruptcy are not foolproof, and sometimes a seemingly endangered company will manage to stay afloat and even prosper. One example that comes quickly to mind is Meshulam Riklis' Rapid-American Corporation. There was a time in the early 1960s when the company showed every sign of going under. There was a myriad of lawsuits, divisions were being sold off, the stock was falling out of bed, but a remarkable earnings recovery at McCrory Corporation, one of R-A's major holdings, seemed to turn the entire complex around, and now the Riklis empire is making nothing but money. The Rapid-American case stands out in my mind because I recall collecting clippings of the troublesome developments and building a file for use as background in anticipation of some kind of bankruptcy proceedings. I never got to use the file.

But more often than not, when I started putting together news clippings, the bankruptcy would come through for me.

In seeking out telltale trouble signs, study carefully any announcement of a "restructuring" of debt. Public-relations people work hard and long trying to make financial disaster read like New Year's Eve, and debt restructuring could mean anything from a simple switch of maturities to a 10 percent settlement with creditors. Ignore the rhetoric and look to the substance.

The typical "debt restructuring" letter to stockholders from a financially strapped corporation might go like this:

We are pleased to inform you that discussions with our banks and other major lending institutions have come to a successful conclusion. As a result of these discussions, the maturities on our short-term debt have been extended for three years and the current portion of our long-term debt has also been extended. The lending institutions have agreed to accept subordinated debentures and warrants to purchase 200,000 shares of your company stock.

The notice would go on to give more specifics of the deal and end up by pointing out that this means "your company is now in a position to face the future with an improved financial structure and dramatically increased working capital. We can move ahead with confidence in our continued growth and progress."

Sounds like a buy recommendation from your favorite broker, doesn't it? Well, here's what really happened. "Your company" is flat on its can and didn't have the money to pay off its loans. So the bankers and insurance-company executives got together at a meeting, looked over the figures, turned pale and tried to get a company that needed a tax loss to buy your company and bail them out.

Since things were tough all over, everyone the financial institutions approached either had tax losses of their own or wanted to steal your company. The banks had to find another way out.

So they had another meeting and decided that if they pressed for their money, your company would be pushed into bankruptcy and nobody would get anything, except the lawyers and the accountants. Having nothing to lose, they agreed to defer their debts and hoped a miracle would turn your company around and eventually bring in some money. They subordinated their debt because they knew that was the only way your company could get new credit and stand a chance of survival. Suppliers are generally more sophisticated than the average stockholder and recognize that if your company couldn't pay its bank debt, it might also have trouble paying for merchandise. By subordinating, the banks in effect made a contribution to your company's capital.

As I mentioned, it is the job of public-relations people to disguise the disaster through the manipulation of language. Sometimes they get so carried away they begin believing the stuff themselves.

A PR man I know who handled a red-hot double-knit company fell into just such a trap. He worked his tail off touting his client's growth potential, and for a time the company's stock flew. But then the client ran into problems. Despite all this potential, the company didn't have enough money to pay for the merchandise it bought. But the PR man kept grinding out releases about well-known underwriting firms falling over themselves to raise new millions for the client, and the Eurodollar market was ready to supply more millions and how the losses were over and the future was soaring sales and capital gains. All the while the PR man's own bills to the client piled up unpaid on a desk in the double-knitter's bookkeeping department. Since the client's prospects were so bright, the PR man didn't worry too much about the bills.

When the bankruptcy came, the poor public-relations counselor was hung up for $15,000—a general, unsecured creditor. A proof of claim in the bankruptcy courts has no spaces for euphemisms. You file your claim and wait for years, and most of the time you collect zilch. In this particular case, zilch was assured because all the assets were pledged on loans that had long since been spent.

If you are in business, look askance if there is a sudden change of heart on the part of a potential customer who for years has been steadfastly resisting your sales efforts.

One morning he calls: "Joe," he says, "I think we can do business. I've been thinking for a long time now that we should handle some of your merchandise, and there's no time like the present. Why don't you send one of your salesmen down to see me soon, maybe even this morning?"

You get all excited and dispatch your best salesman down to see him. The salesman comes back with his order book loaded up.

"I can't understand why we had so much trouble selling this boy before; he's a regular cupcake. He took everything in the line—right across the board—every size, every color, every style. Man, I never had such an easy order in my life. My hand hurts from writing so fast."

Two weeks later the cupcake files a Chapter XI petition.

A salesman friend of mine didn't have to wait two weeks. He got the bad news in a couple of days.

He was just learning his trade and beginning to think salesmen were regarded by the outside world as sub-human. Why did resident buying offices have these beautiful reception rooms for clients and dark, dingy doors down the hall marked "salesmen's entrance"? Why did everyone seem to be avoiding him?

As his morale was about to hit bottom, he walked into a store with his sample case and was greeted like a visiting diplomat from the Court of St. James.

"Come in. Sit down. Can we get you some coffee? Let me take your coat."

He was invited to show his line and spent the entire afternoon writing up the biggest order he had ever seen. This was on a Friday. On Monday he opened the *Daily News Record* and there at the head of the "Business Troubles" column was an item about a bankruptcy petition filed by this sonofabitch who had so generously ordered everything in the line.

The point is, if the sale is too easy, worry. When Billie Sol Estes, convicted of fraud in 1964, was making the rounds of New York finance companies selling mortgages on phantom fertilizer tanks, one of the few firms that turned him away did so because "the bride was too beautiful." The deal Billie Sol was offering was too sweet and the price too good.

"Why would he be coming to me with this kind of deal? I should be chasing after him" was the way the finance-company executive thought, and that spared him the honor of being mentioned among some of the nation's top names in Billie Sol's list of creditors.

The withdrawal of a proposed bond issue because of "market conditions" is deserving of a suspicious glance. Lots of perfectly sound companies withdraw issues because interest rates have gone up too fast or for some other reason unrelated to financial difficulties. But "unfavorable market conditions" can be another way of saying, "Nobody in his right mind would buy this paper."

Grayson-Robinson Stores and Beck Industries both withdrew bond issues before turning to the bankruptcy courts, and in each case "unfavorable market conditions" were cited. It just so happens that market conditions *were* unfavorable—Grayson-Robinson was a victim of the stock-market slump of May 1962 and Beck Industries was caught in the 1969–70 debacle. But both companies were already in trouble when they tried to raise the new money from the public, and when the bond issues flopped they were forced into bankruptcy proceedings.

Accounting discrepancies should also start the bells ringing in your head. If a company delays issuing its figures because auditors are reviewing the records or if the company issues figures and then withdraws them for revision, watch it. The revisions will almost surely spell bad news.

Remember Ecological Sciences Corporation? The first sign of trouble came when the SEC got a little miffed about a utility passing itself off as an environmental-protection company. But the clincher hit when the firm's accounting practices were questioned. It wasn't long before a Chapter XI petition was filed by Eco's subsidiary, Ecological Utilities, Inc.

Sheffield Watch Corporation was another firm that issued a number of press releases about audit delays shortly before taking a trip to the bankruptcy courts.

A further example of accounting problems being the forerunner of more serious developments was the Botany Industries case. When Botany, one of the nation's largest manufacturers of men's clothing, filed its figures for fiscal 1971 with the SEC and the American Stock Exchange, the firm's auditors added a disclaimer that rendered the report virtually meaningless. The accountants questioned some specific items such as the adequacy of reserves to cover losses from the liquidation of subsidiaries and even questioned whether it was "appropriate" to treat the company as a "going concern" for accounting purposes.

About four months later, on April 25, 1972, Botany and its subsidiary, H. Daroff & Sons, filed Chapter XI petitions in Federal court, Philadelphia.

A public denial by a company that it is having financial difficulties is one of the surest signs that the company is in the soup. In fact, I've developed my own denial index. I add two points to it every time the company denies it's in trouble, and before the denials add up to ten the chances are the company is in a lawyer's office working up the bankruptcy papers.

Vague statements about extraordinary write-offs can also tip off deeper trouble. On December 27, 1968, Mill Factors Corporation, a publicly owned factoring and commercial finance company, issued the following press release:

Mill Factors Corporation announced today that developments as to certain of its clients in its Commercial Finance

Division would probably require that the Corporation at the year end establish reserves or effect write offs with respect to amounts owed to the corporation by such clients. Investigations and analyses presently being conducted have not yet reached the stage where it is possible to determine the final amount of such reserves or write offs. However, it is expected that they will more than offset the earnings that would otherwise have been reported for the year 1968 and create some amount of deficit for 1968 operations.

As it turned out, the write-offs came to about $40 million. The company's entire capital was $11 million. Furthermore, an investigative audit by S. D. Leidesdorf & Company disclosed that had proper reserves been taken, Mill Factors would have been insolvent as far back as December 1965.

The Mill Factors case was kept out of court because its $70 million in debts were concentrated in a relatively small number of banks and insurance companies who agreed to cooperate. After several years of negotiating, the firm's assets were sold to James Talcott, Inc., and there was a pro-rata distribution to creditors. Stockholders were paid a nominal sum to buy their cooperation.

Resignations in high places can be an indication that all is not well. Be especially wary if there is a steady stream of executives leaving a company at the same time operating losses are being reported.

What the PR people are representing as "a strengthening of top-level management" may add up to the old sinking-ship syndrome.

Operating losses are, of course, a standard danger signal. While there are some companies that can go on for years absorbing losses, the more aggressive merger artists generally operate on a thin capital base and can be dumped over by one bad year.

The place to look for next year's busts is in this year's glamour companies. It's axiomatic in the bankruptcy business that whatever line of business catches fire on Wall Street will soon be fattening the insolvency experts.

In the 1967–68 bull market, the biggest winners were the electronics and computer companies, nursing homes and leasing firms. More recently, the Street has been strong on double-knit companies.

The roster of electronics- and computer-firm failures is formidable—Visual Electronics, Polarad Electronics, Federated Purchaser, Inc., Milo Electronics, Comtel Corporation, Decitron Electronics, Computer Applications, Brandon Applied Systems, Farrington—the list goes on.

Four Seasons Nursing Homes, the most famous of the health-care operations, slipped into bankruptcy proceedings. Bermec Corporation, a leasing company that dabbled in tax-sheltered cattle raising, had a good run on Wall Street before bankruptcy proceedings intervened. The double-knitters are beginning to go under, and you can be sure there will be more. And if pornography continues growing at its current pace, that will be the area to look for the next great bankruptcy wave.

Finally, beware of fancy annual reports. If AT&T puts out an expensive-looking brochure with lots of slick illustrations, that's O.K. Telephone can afford it. But if Cockabolly Industries comes out with a report in glorious color with inserts and pullouts and page after page of pretty girls smiling happily, get suspicious. This company is PRing its stock, so better take a careful look at the numbers, especially the footnotes.

The most beautiful annual report I ever saw was the 1969 issue of National Student Marketing Corporation. The layouts were impeccable and the copy sheer poetry. Too bad these standards of excellence weren't matched by the figures.

As Andrew Tobias, a former NSMC vice-president, points out in his book about his adventures with the company, the NSMC financial statement for the year ended August 31, 1969, contained a "killer footnote" showing that $3,754,103, or substantially all the company's profits that year, came by grinding in earnings of companies acquired after the close of the accounting period.

Under the pooling-of-interest concept of accounting for mergers, this was acceptable procedure for handling the transactions. However, as the result of abuses by NSMC and other merger-happy concerns, the accounting profession has since tightened up its rules governing the treatment of acquisitions.

In recognizing early warnings of trouble, the trick is to separate the public relations from the realities. The victim of any con job, be it a stock promotion or a bankruptcy hustle, is really a victim of his own greed. If the bride is too beautiful, the groom should expect to get a good screwing.